THE AFRO FANTASY WALKING TREE ORACLE

Plant Allies, Ancestor Magic, and Healing
through Ritual and Ceremony

MONTICUE CONNALLY

WITH ART BY JONATHON STALLS

North Atlantic Books
Huichin, unceded Ohlone land
Berkeley, California

Published by
North Atlantic Books
Huichin, unceded Ohlone land
Berkeley, California

Art by Jonathon Stalls
Cover design by Jasmine Hromjak
Book design by Happenstance Type-O-Rama
Printed in China

The Afro Fantasy Walking Tree Oracle: Plant Allies, Ancestor Magic, and Healing through Ritual and Ceremony is sponsored and published by North Atlantic Books, an educational nonprofit based in the unceded Ohlone land Huichin (Berkeley, CA) that collaborates with partners to develop cross-cultural perspectives; nurture holistic views of art, science, the humanities, and healing; and seed personal and global transformation by publishing work on the relationship of body, spirit, and nature.

North Atlantic Books's publications are distributed to the US trade and internationally by Penguin Random House Publisher Services. For further information, visit our website at www.northatlanticbooks.com.

ISBN: 979-8-88984-231-6

1 2 3 4 5 6 7 8 9 ASIA PACIFIC 29 28 27 26 25

North Atlantic Books is committed to the protection of our environment. We print on recycled paper whenever possible and partner with printers who strive to use environmentally responsible practices.

CONTENTS

The Royal Court

About the Author

INTRODUCTION

I am an African American shaman, medium, and herbalist with blood ties to the Fulani tribe of Senegal, the Yoruba tribe of Nigeria, foundational Black Americans, the island of Barbados, and the lands of Morocco. Each cultural thread brings so much to who I am, and I'm honored to be able to rebuild these links after the damage that was done through the horrific transatlantic slave trade, the colonization of the Americas, and the lies attached to being constantly reshaped and reclassified by outside forces into false tribes such as "Negro" or "Colored" to separate us from our powerful origins.

Right relationships that existed between us and familiar natural spaces were developed for thousands of years and then violently cleared out through genocide and the displacement of people from their Indigenous lands. Those right relationships are just as valuable as the minerals, plants, and sunlight, and when our people were killed or removed, that soil and the spirits of those lands also suffered, and in some places dried up completely. When the right relationships are lost, the dreams become distorted. We can see the destruction all throughout lands where this has happened—and the physical realm is not the only realm that suffers. The Earth yearns for human indigeneity and connection, and Blackness should always be a tool used for digging into the rich darkness of the Akashic Mother for our best dreams. We must use the useful bits of history and also study all of our lasting earth peoples to pull out the most necessary and medicinal cultural practices for the people. What even is Blackness without a cultural connection to the practices that made it great and medicinal?

AFRO FANTASY AS MEDICINE

Before I was able to find my own ancestral cultural links, in order to spiritually connect to a Blackness that wasn't defined or shaped as a response to whiteness, I relied upon the often-vague stories from my grandparents, and the "far out" stories of Afro Fantasy and Afrofuturist authors such as Octavia Butler, Nnedi Okorafor, and Ayi Kwei Armah to feed my spirit. We, as a people, are so blessed to have access to the many books and short stories of Afro Fantasy that pull the reader into worlds where what we know to be Blackness can expand beyond mainstream notions and realities.

Speaking of Afro Fantasy, it's important to note that fantasies aren't "fake." Fantasies are real, being false only to people who lack the vision or sensitivity to grasp their potential, power, and realness. Prophets and seers are the carriers of powerful fantasies that will reveal expansive truths that grow into the life-altering events of tomorrow. A powerful mass paradigm shift can turn a fantasy into a physical reality in an instant. Fantasies are "fake" to people already invested in the fantasies they were often born into. They call their beloved fantasies facts or reality. The truth is that fantasies are real. They are possibilities, real paths, real revelations, and real seeds being planted into space-time through our words and the behaviors they inspire within us. Every religion, invention, business, or romance began as a fantasy in the heart and mind of someone impregnated with it.

To catch a break from the onslaught of mainstream Western assumptions, fantasies, and attitudes toward Blackness that wanted to limit my mind in ways that only benefit some diabolical money machine or racist caste system, I often turned within with the aid of mystical tools. I searched for meaning and context in regards to my own relationship with Blackness through working with tarot decks, especially decks that centered their theme and purpose around people of color. In contrast to the endless array of both "real-world" and symbolic white authority figures that surrounded me, it was only in those African-centered decks that I was ever influenced by a Black African king, even if he was a humble King of Cups!

Someone at this point may ask: What's the point of having access to a King of Cups?! What's the point in having some fictional tarot card king? What's the point of all these Afro Fantastic worlds? Aren't these worlds just secular, nonspiritual worlds that exist for escape and enjoyment? My answers to these questions may shock some. **Nothing** is secular or devoid of spirit. Everything in the universe is composed of, or serves in the feeding of, some spirit. We exist in a spiritual jungle and this jungle is hungry. We've been fooled into thinking that a stroll in the park, for example, is an activity devoid of a religious or spiritual nature, because we aren't truly taught what is. There is a spirit in the air, a spirit in the trees and even in the grasses caressing your feet. We participate in rituals all the time and don't know it. Think of all the people who leave out cookies for a spirit named Santa Claus or those who enjoy birthday parties where a flame is sacrificed to bring in the new season. Spirit is everywhere. Many spirits are attached to stories and patterns and even smells. They are attracted to emotions as well, and we humans are never short of them. Our ancestors are spirits very concerned with our lives, often suggesting or even riding our fantasies right into an existing future. Our fantasies are real and divine and filled with a powerful Asé that must be respected.

It's important at this point to assert that "fiction" doesn't exist. The *idea* of fiction **does** exist, but fiction itself does not. Everything is real somewhere. There are nine realms of existence, and they all affect us for better or worse based on who we are and where we are trying to go. Everything is real, but there is a sliding scale of how impactful or important a reality is for you. If you have opened these pages, you are either a Black Afro Dreamer who is ready for the resurrection of true ancestral Black power or one of a culturally and racially diverse array of spitfire magical allies in the struggle to unlearn the distortion programming, knowing that there is a clear link between the suppression of the spiritually gifted masses, the restoration of the land, and the oppression of people of color.

When I was a young American Black child idolizing the sounds, dances, and ever-brightening skin color of Michael Jackson, my mother came to me one day and shifted my paradigm. She placed within me the idea of a strong Black nation. She told me that we had become members of the Nation of Islam. It was under this tradition that I learned that being Black was a divine thing and that the UFOs that everyone was talking about were actually being operated by angelic brown-skinned, curly haired beings just like me. Sure, this may sound like science fiction to some, but as a child, I felt so protected and empowered under this new fantasy. Confidence, security, and other very real changes came into my life because of it! Even after my family left the Nation when I was thirteen, I never stopped searching and reading in order to propel myself out of what I perceived to be a racist and dry fantasy I'd been born into called the United States.

Similarly, the movie *Django Unchained* pushed minds into fantasies that imagined Black people in ways they hadn't seen before on the big screen. This movie told us that Black people were never just some oppressed people of beatings, praying, and running for freedom. We always knew that we were "good" people. But *Django Unchained* told us that we are both good *and* beautifully dangerous. This fantasy, a so-called fictional story, became a bridge propelling us into a truth that was very important. Black people can't ever be completely oppressed, because we have sharp teeth just like the oppressors! In the past and up until now, we've always been actively fighting like hell! The stories of the many victories we have taken through force are not told. Black people are fierce and magical.

American Black truths such as these have been suppressed in order to maintain the power of the current American dream. The "fictional" movie *Django Unchained* holds more truth than the popular American whitewashed history books, because it planted the seeds that led to the awareness of the many wars and rebellions that happened throughout the Americas and the West Indies that led to strong Maroon societies and successful Black-owned towns. *Django Unchained* carries very real seeds to our American past while also bringing out the warrior genius potential in the present that will become our collective future.

Our oppression is only as strong as the successful suppression of our healing stories. We as a people must get to a point where we are always aware of where the so-called facts are coming from. When these "facts" don't feed our spirits, we must look to the truths still alive in our so-called myths, so-called fictional stories, and dreams. Our truths must be living, teeming with life, and breathing power into our collective dream. Sometimes we need to stop learning facts and start resonating with power. "Facts" are not inherently beneficial, because even ideas that appear to be facts have been delivered in ways that do harm. It is of greater benefit to see what is happening *around* a proposed fact than to blindly worship an idea just because it's called a fact by some supposed authority. I remember when teachers would teach young Black kids about the importance of vitamin D. They'd say, "Vitamin D is essential for strong bones, so always drink your milk." But the majority of African Americans are lactose intolerant. We must actively dream ourselves out of oppressive programming in order to be powerful and healthy.

It's also important to note that it's often the things we don't believe in that hurt us the most. So, Monticue, are you saying that Superman is real? Yes. He exists in many realms and affects our reality. He exists in our mental spaces very strongly, being able to randomly pop up into our thoughts for inspiration or entertainment. We can also have a full-on conversation with him in the dream space (a.k.a. the Astral Realm) as well. On Halloween, he even exists physically through the people who wear his costumes in his honor. Can he exist strongly in the Physical Realm as a flying alien man who shoots lasers out of his eyes? No. This is not possible in the Physical Realm. Of course, that doesn't mean a person like him doesn't physically exist somewhere in the universe. The point here is that all probabilities can't manifest perfectly in every plane, but that doesn't take away from their realness. The same concept goes for the Black King of Water or Air or Earth or Fire that pops up within this oracle! They can be just as influential or even more so, pushing the energy of Black pride, power, imagination, and appreciation. These oracular entities are living and breathing within you! So speak to them when they appear! Use your mind's eye to give gifts, build relationships, and benefit from their wisdom.

WALKING TREES

This Afro Fantasy Walking Tree Oracle deck is a tool built to rebuild and restore respectful relations with the natural world both inside and outside the reader. Nature is an intelligent multidimensional time matrix made up of seen and unseen living parts. This nature I speak of, and its seen and unseen parts, are reflected in our human bodies, for we are also composed of the seen and unseen. For example, you may see my face when I am speaking to you, but you can't directly see my thoughts or my soul. The human body is also representative of nature, in that the body holds specific centers of concentrated healing and creative power. Our own beating hearts are great examples of this, in that great healing can come from wrapping our arms around loved ones, pulling them close, and touching the concentrated power of our heart with theirs. The heart of our Mama Nature can be experienced through interfacing with the mountains, forests, plants, trees, and animal sightings; and we are fundamentally designed to heal through innately connecting to the bosom of Mama Nature.

The two-part, rhythmic "lub dub" sound of our hearts that takes place as we calmly move through time reflects the two-part, "left, right" step of a human as they move through space. In this way, walking is a type of heartbeat. The sounds of rhythmic footsteps and also heartbeats are sounds of motion. Meditating on our own heart rhythms and deep breathing can move us to deeper paths within. Intentional walking is a way of connecting to our own hearts and also to the heart of the forest. In other words, when we are moving through natural spaces in a meditative way, we are hugging the heart of the forest.

The trees, plants, streams, and all of nature's children are always eager to work with us. These pure manifested aspects of the Earth's heart pull us into harmony with a much larger expression of natural power. This power is also a magnifier for the natures that exist within each and every one of us.

One of the absolutely most potent magnifiers and energizers on earth are the trees. Our subtle energy bodies can merge with fields of trees and be expanded and powered up in ways that can produce miraculous healing. If modern people could truly slow down and feel how much power that a tree generates, they would be in absolute awe of the giant earth angels we walk past every day. When we are touching our own heart to the tree, which is a direct extension of the Earth's heart, a bridge is made. A piece of that tree spirit merges with that of your heart. When you walk away from that tree with which you've built intimacy and relationship, its spirit, now being a part of you, rooted in your aura, walks wherever you go. It becomes a **Walking Tree**.

This is why the Walking Tree Oracle asks the reader to walk slowly and intentionally through parks or other green spaces so that the beings in nature, often connected to trees and other natural bodies such as streams, lakes, and stones, can make themselves more readily available. It is sometimes suggested to connect with an element of physical nature in order to fully activate the power of the oracle card you are working with. The card you pull from this deck will activate a healing force within and will often guide you to meditate with a tree or some other element of nature. We can't expect the mysteries of nature to open up to us if we don't regularly check in with, open up to, and have a working relationship with the power centers of nature as manifested through plants and streams and forests.

ANSWERING THE CALL

All Black Indigenous systems have had an intimate and practical connection to nature. It was through divination systems, ceremonies, dreams, and other spiritual technologies that the Lords of Nature were given a direct voice in the community. These beings were welcomed because the Indigenous people had a sense of reverence and respect for these spirits. Not following a proper protocol with nature spirits could throw off these beings and their work, which could ultimately throw off the balance of nature. Allowing the balance to fall to pieces could bring in dangerous forces. These dangerous forces could make the land sick or even manifest as illness in the bodies of humans. It was essential for humans to ask for permission before moving in certain ways so as not to be disrespectful to the guardians of nature. Asking for permission is decolonization. This Walking Tree Oracle deck is a direct link to elemental energies of the forest, our ancestry, our future, and the many realms in between. This deck was inspired by my experience with nine realms of existence, the traditional tarot, herbalism, African traditional religion, and astrology.

The old ways are calling us to get back to the future sooner rather than later. Our Black future is filled with deep and unbreakable connections to Mother Earth and the Lords of Nature. But we must be willing to find the right stories that build faith in ourselves, our communities, and our most prophetically and psychically talented. We see so much but there is so much we can't see.

For example, many people don't believe in, or even have knowledge of the existence of, dust mites, but they are there living on the beds of some people. For some people living with dust mites, the bugs can cause eye redness or sneezing or other indirect effects. But there's a rare group of people so sensitive that they can feel the dust mites crawling on them directly. The same goes for the spirits. Some people can't sense them at all consciously, whereas the sensitives can sense a quite obvious energy shift right on the skin. This oracle deck will give you tools to read that realm and better understand and commune with nature.

Afrofuturism is about dreaming, seeing, and prophesying through a reimagined Black lens. It is truly healing our hearts, helping us to envision a world where we exist in futures both near and far with all of our Blackness intact—Africoid features, traditionally Black hairstyles and hair textures, styles of dress, ways of speaking, ways of praying, ways of resonating, ways of responding to rhythms, African drum beats, hip-hop patterns, chants, orisha spirits, gospel music, and all things that Blackness can perceive. Let us envision a future where we can reincarnate and still recognize our Black selves in every way and in all nine realms. Let's wish for our offspring to look inside and outside themselves and see our Black radiance shining back at them.

.. .

Let's envision a Black future that includes the safety and preservation of beautiful Black bodies, minds, vibrations, incantations, and traits as carrying vessels. Let's see them as containers carrying our biggest natural cures and spirit medicines from the past into the now. Let's see them move from the now into the future. Let's see them move from a Black future that can activate sacred space and carry medicine into the past while also influencing how we perceive that past. The past is a mysterious container that is altered by the stories and lighting shone upon it. The way the Black past informs the Black future should always be healing. In our sacred sciences, we know that the future and the past can both be influenced by the now. The ways we move today influence and shape the future. Colors shone into the past from the future can influence how medicinal a story becomes in the present.

Let's imagine a Black future where all our containers reinforce those patterns that would support a Black nation in the best ways. A future where all our entertainment and art and music and mathematics and religion truly reinforce strong Black families, which are the foundation for any strong and thriving Black tribes or nations. Nations have the power to protect themselves while moving in states of boldness and beauty.

Let's imagine a future where Black nations have full and unsupervised access to the ancient temples linked to their stories and their own DNA. A future where the genius of Black antiquity does not rest in the profiting hands of colonial museums. Let's dream of a Black future where no one can take what is historically and rightfully Black. A Black future where Black tribal magicians who are sovereign and untouchable can walk into a museum and take what they need back to the sacred tombs. Let's dream of a future where Black nations take all of their shit back so they can work their magic at their sacred sites. Imagine that. Real Black mystics at the Great Pyramid of Giza with their animals and herbal mixtures spraying rum and blowing tobacco smoke onto ancient shrines. Imagine circles of Black masses around the Great Sphinx, chanting and sending energy through the sphinx as a portal into a Black future. Imagine a Black future where the West African religions of our ancestors are celebrated and not widely expressed through media outlets as witchcraft or devil worship.

Imagine a Black future where ancient initiation and spiritual recognition systems are intact. Let's envision a world full of culturally celebrated rites of passage ceremonies for Black folk that honor major changes that come about in a human life—magical rites that simultaneously call in spirits that activate DNA for proper integration and psycho-spiritual development. Imagine a Black future that is able to recognize its healers, its prophets, and its mages at birth (or some critical point in childhood) and whisk them away to have those gifts developed in service to the family, tribe, and environment. Let us use this Afro Fantasy Walking Tree Oracle to its fullest and most medicinal capacities. Let us dream the impossible dreams and never cease until our current landscape shifts to match that shining vision!

Asé!

HOW TO USE THIS DECK

The Walking Tree Oracle is in some ways structurally built like a traditional tarot deck. This was done so a tarot reader could feel right at home, being able to pull extra meaning from traditional tarot lore while reading the oracle. There are, however, major differences from traditional tarot. One key difference is the use of the number 33 for the Major Arcana instead of 22. The number 33 was chosen to harness the powers of enlightenment, creative power, and also the mysteries associated with this master number. Aside from the large image on a card, one can also pull meaning from the smaller astrological and planetary symbols on a card. Cards also indicate one of nine realms that they correspond to. Read more on those in "The Nine Realms" section of this book.

To get the most from this deck, you'll want to read the book in its entirety and keep it close as a reference guide. Does that mean that you must read the book before you can start the readings? Of course not! Start your readings today and use the "Cards and Descriptions" section to look at deeper card meanings, ritual guidance, and visual meditations as you go!

MAIN SPREADS

Whenever cards are laid in a particular way for reading, this is known as a "spread." It is easy to focus on the cards themselves, but spreads aren't often considered enough for their own innate power. There is actual power in the number of cards pulled and also the shape the cards pulled end up in. So be intentional with the spreads you choose, and don't be afraid to experiment and create spreads that inspire you. A few of the main spreads are listed below.

PREPARING TO READ YOUR AFRO FANTASY WALKING TREE ORACLE

Pour a cup of water and light a candle.
Still the mind and stare into the water as the light flickers through it. State your intention.

A SIMPLE ONE-CARD SPREAD

Shuffle the deck and set it down on the table. Pull one card from the top. Place that one card on the table, propped up where you can see it. In the "Cards and Descriptions" section of this book, read the "Practice" section of the description for the card, and imagine yourself performing that practice. If the practice is an outdoor practice, make a plan for when you can go perform the ritual. You may want to do the ritual related to the card a number of times throughout the month. Take note of the herb assigned to the card, and consider working with it in some capacity. Also take note of the realm associated with the card. The realm will tell you where the root of the problem is.

TWO ROADS SPREAD

The Two Roads Spread is for someone in a quick jam. If a person has 5–10 minutes to make a difficult decision, they can use this spread to lay two cards representing two clear roads. One card leads to success, and the other is not so fortunate.

Shuffle the cards and break the deck on the table into three stacks from left to right. Pull two cards from the center stack. Place one to the left and one to the right. The card on the left represents the direction you should not go. The card on the right represents the proper path. Read the description in the book, perform the ritual, and move in the way you are guided.

INVERTED PYRAMID SPREAD

The Inverted Pyramid Spread carries great power, depth, and precision. Its pyramid shape moves facing downward, acting like a drill to get to what lies beneath the surface. The inverted pyramid is designed in a way that allows the reader to quickly receive deep and clear answers on what to do for very specific problems that arise.

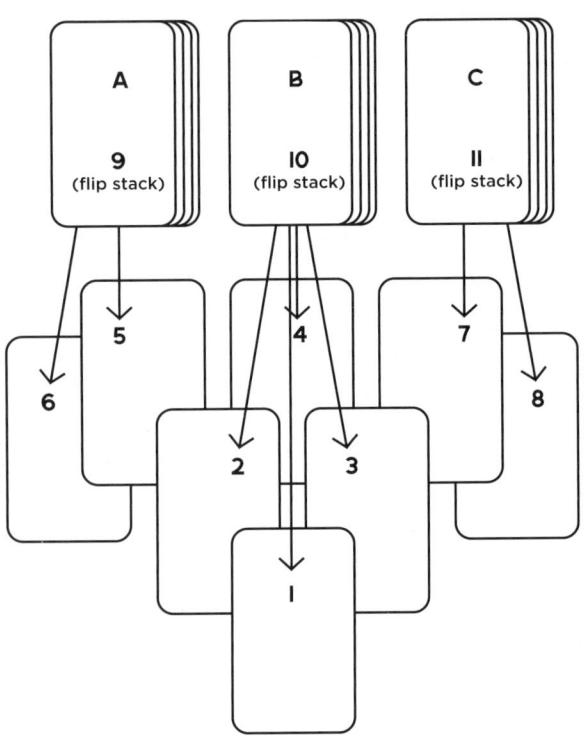

Shuffle the cards and place them into three stacks. This spread is designed to look like an upside-down pyramid when all the cards are pulled. Pull a card from the middle stack a three-card distance toward you and flip that card. That card represents how the ancestors see you.

Pull two more cards from the middle stack, and place them diagonally to the left and right of the first card. The second card, which is on the left, represents how people see you; and the one on the right represents how you are really feeling. Pull another card from the middle stack, and place it right in front of the middle stack. This card represents the overall message of the spread. Pull one card from the left stack to see the "what not to do" card. Next, pull a secondary card from the same stack and slide it partially underneath that card to contribute to its meaning. Pull a card from the stack on the right to see the "what you *should* do" card. Pull another card from the same stack and slide it partially underneath that card to support it. Flip the three stacks to see the past, present, and future of the situation. Upside-down cards are not considered reversed in this spread. All cards are read as if upright.

OVERALL SPREAD

The Overall Spread is a very complete and important fundamental spread. It allows for much longer sessions that help the reader to see into many healing themes that will bring balance to the client. The spread moves like a snake that will eventually bite its own tail. Based in numerology, each position where a card is placed is synced with the energy of that number, making for a rich and informative session.

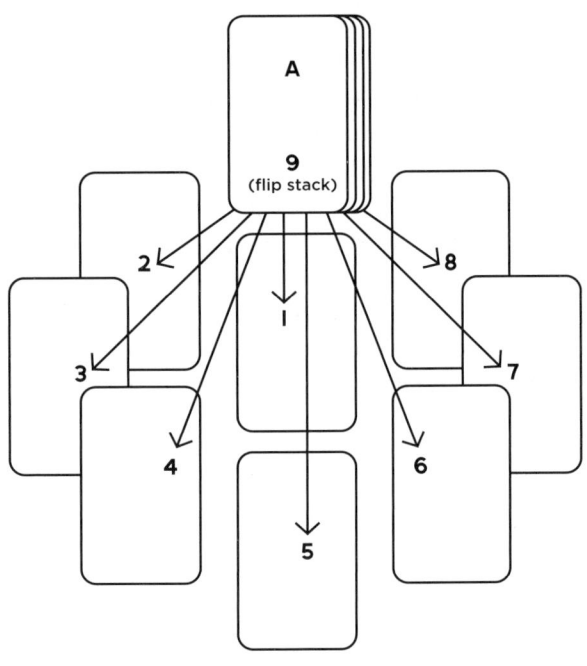

The first card pulled represents you. The second card pulled from the stack represents how you should approach your love life. The third card pulled represents how you should approach your creative projects. The fourth card represents how you should approach your job or mundane money hustles. The fifth card represents what you should stop doing. The sixth card represents how you should approach family or close friends during the current season.

The seventh card represents what your primary focus should be. The eighth card represents the future. Flip the whole shuffled stack over. That card represents the overall message. Upside-down cards are not considered reversed in this spread. All cards are read as if upright.

THE SEATS SPREAD

The Seats Spread is based on the idea that there are specific seats of power in the mind. Each seat is a position in your own mind that attracts and then promotes the person sitting in it. For example, everyone has a Romance seat, a throne ready to attract and promote a love interest. The card pulled into this position will show a reader who they naturally draw in romantically. There are seven seats in total: Romance, Father, Mother, Best Friend, Student, Enemy, and Savior. Some of the seats will have living people sitting in them already. You also may notice during a reading that the others are empty.

In order to perform this spread, shuffle the cards and pull seven cards from the shuffled deck. The one you pulled first is the seat of Romance, the second is the Father, and so on all the way to the last card, which is the Savior. These cards show you either who is sitting in the seat, who should be sitting in that seat, how you should treat who is sitting in the seat, or how to attract someone to sit in the seat and play the role you need them to play.

Romance	This seat is the seat of the person you're destined to romantically love in this life.
Father	This seat is the seat of the person you look to for protection and help with money matters.
Mother	This is the seat of the person you look to, to nurture you and bless your heart.
Best Friend	This is the seat of the person you can confide in.
Student	This is the seat of the students you are supposed to reach.
Enemy	This is the seat of a trickster who has only thrown obstacles in your path.
Savior	This is the seat of your greatest mentor and true path.

For example, let's say you pull the Princess of Air as your Romance card. It could mean that your romantic partners will tend to be very emotional, somewhat immature, hot-headed, playful, and assertive.

CARD FEATURES

NINE REALMS MEDICINE

The multiverse of which we are a part is made of nine realms: the Nighttime Object Realm, the Physical Realm, the Ethereal Realm, the Astral Realm, the Mental Realm, the Intuitive Realm, the Ancestral Realm, the

Coincidence Realm, and the Mythic Realm. Each realm holds keys to our health and the ways our energies naturally move through time-space. A great feature of this deck is that the user can directly ask from which realm the root of their problem is stemming and be directed to either the Mental, Physical, Ancestral, or one of the other six realms. Knowing the realm where a problem or illness is rooted is the best hint to how to remedy it. The Walking Tree Oracle will tell you exactly which realm the disease is stemming from. For example, if you know that the disease is rooted in the Mental Realm, you know that the primary medicines should cater toward it. If the core is not addressed and this person only chemically treats the body (Physical Realm) to remedy the situation, the illness is not truly cured, only suppressed. Suppressed illnesses always find a way eventually. So, you'll want to identify the primary realm of the illness so that you can select your primary medicines. Secondary medicines can also help support the workings from other realms. Here is another example: If someone is having nightmares, there are many potential causes. A nightmare can be caused by eating certain foods too late at night (Physical Realm), emotional distress (Astral Realm), mental distress (Mental Realm), ancestral curses (Ancestral Realm), evil objects in the home (Nighttime Object Realm), and so on. Each oracle card holds a realm symbol representing the realm with which the card correlates.

REVERSED CARDS

There are times while reading the cards in this deck that cards can take on the opposite meaning. When a card's meaning shifts to its opposite, that card is "reversed." There are descriptions of card reversal meanings as part of each card description. If the reader pulls a card and it lands upside down while reading, its opposite meaning should be considered. If the reader pulls a card that ends up in the negative part of a spread, the reversed meaning should be considered.

RITUALS AND HERBAL BASICS

The rituals in this book are here to create sacred space portals that allow only the most well-meaning, wise, and powerful beings to enter our space while reading cards. Plants are meditation and prayer magnifiers, so they will always be recommended in the space. It's important to note here that each card has a specific herb or set of herbs that corresponds to it. So if you are drawing one card, you can lay it down and then read the description of that card in the book to get the ritual details and the recommended herbs. Always pray or sing over herbs and state your intention. The general dosage is a tablespoon of herb per cup of water. Do not take these herbs in a capsule. I would prefer for readers to use either a small strainer ball or a strainer spoon filled with leaves and/or flowers in a cup of freshly boiled water. Leave the herbs to steep for at least

15 minutes. It is also a good idea to use a French press. For roots and barks, add them to boiling water in a pot and reduce the heat to a simmer for at least 15 minutes before drinking. If you planted herbs in your garden, don't be afraid to use them for the suggested teas. If you are harvesting from the forest, make sure you take a skilled herbalist with you to make sure you don't pick any poisons. You can also buy these herbs from your local apothecary or online apothecaries. Mountain Rose has some high-quality herbs. If you know plants in your region and notice that any of their energies match the vibration of these cards, please substitute as needed.

PLANETARY AND ZODIAC CORRESPONDENCE

Each card in the deck corresponds to a planet and a zodiac sign. Allow the mysteries and meanings around them to add to your oracle reading experience. The zodiac and the planets add extra richness to an already powerful oracle deck. Note that each zodiac sign and each planet also represent a relationship within the body. The zodiac sign represents an area of the body or a body system. For example, Aries represents the head from the nose up. The planet represents a force and how it affects that area. For example, a few of the forces Mars represents are accidents, inflammation, or excess heat. Therefore, if you look at your astrological chart or two cards you've pulled and see "Mars in Aries," you may want to watch for accidents to the head!

GOING DEEPER

The following sections are for readers who want to go deeper into the theory and hidden worlds that operate behind the Afro Fantasy Walking Tree Oracle deck and its creation. This section adds to the practical versatility of how you, the reader, can use this oracle deck for purposes of deep spiritual healing. Those mysteriously drawn to this oracle are being called to pull close to these materials in order to become a full-fledged Walking Tree Oracle Practitioner, one who is able to effectively move deeper and deeper into a rich relationship with the Afro Fantasy Walking Tree Oracle. This is done in order to connect to the best parts of our multidimensional selves while becoming an agent of healing in relation to community, the ancestors, and the mysterious powers of nature.

THE NINE REALMS

REALM 1, THE NIGHTTIME OBJECT REALM

Realm 1, the **Nighttime Object Realm**, is the dark realm of the conscious living aspects of darkness that move and that create numerous portals into this reality. This realm is the link that ties magic to specific inanimate, dead, or slow-moving physical beings such as living plants, parts of plants, bones, types of dolls, and charmed objects. It is important to know that both beneficial and nonbeneficial beings exist in this realm. A deeper truth is that the souls of all living beings must briefly pass through this dark realm like a dark cosmic womb, to have a working physical body and a destiny. A soul must also pass through this realm on the way out. The layer of a person that is the animated living shadow of the person remains with the bones at death.

There are also beings that must pass through the realm in a specific magical way to attach to nonliving objects and therefore charm them. The source of this realm is lunar and dark in nature. The plants know it well because they move at a much slower pace and have roots under the earth in full darkness.

There are regular shadows in this world that spawn from light bouncing off objects, but the shadows of charmed or charged objects are *living* shadows. The living shadows of this realm have powers and wants and are limited by daylight. In daylight they are confined to the shape of the object to which they are tied. The living shadows can expand and become animated at night or sometimes in the absence of light. If you are working with beings and spirits of this plane, they are awake fully when the sun goes down. Light weakens their influence, so I don't recommend performing magic with beings of this realm during the day.

Someone battling a negative being from this realm can often get rid of it by removing the object that being is attached to. A person can also bring a stronger, more positive object, shrine, or plant into the home for protection. When a person performs magic, it is often the fusion of many realms working together. Realm 1, the Nighttime Object Realm, deals with making sure the proper herbs, bones, and so forth, or *ingredients* layer, is correct. The Mental Realm and the emotional Astral Realm add the *intention* layer, and the *ritual* layer makes sure that right rituals pulled from the Coincidence, Ancestral, and Mythic Realms are sound.

Realm 1, the Nighttime Object Realm, is the key to the nighttime beings that work through nature. These shadowy beings are connected to physical objects of power such as bones, fresh roots, fresh tree branches with leaves attached, activated shrines, some paintings, some statues, some dolls, and charmed jewelry.

Spirits: Beings attached to physical objects that have more power at night such as trees, tree branches, strong roots, dolls, paintings, spiritual shrines, and correctly charged objects

REALM 2, THE PHYSICAL REALM

Realm 2, the **Physical Realm**, is the place of physical bodies and those lessons associated with survival and a physical experience. This is the domain of chemicals and substances. If the problem is rooted in this plane, specific medications or herbal constituents or minerals or drinking water will usually do the trick. This is the realm of matter over mind. If you are being led to this realm as an investigative starting point, you may be lacking a mineral in your diet, or the right chemical component. This realm showing up can also point toward needing more physical touch in your life. All these potentials must be addressed to increase functional cohesion in other realms.

Spirits: The spirits of the organs in the body: heart, liver, and others

REALM 3, THE ETHEREAL REALM

Realm 3, the **Ethereal Realm**, is the domain of the subtle ethereal body, the spiritual double of the physical body. This realm is an energetic and nourishing cup that slowly pours valuable energy from the higher realms into the physical body. The Ethereal is the realm of prana or qi or life force. The measure of life force within the body is determined by one's ability to collect and sustain this force in daily life. This realm is strengthened in a person through eating life-filled foods, Daoist seminal retention, and proper movement. It's important to note here that the *energy* of the food you eat is more important in this realm than actual constituents within the food. Chemical and mineral components within a physical body correspond to the Physical Realm. Qigong, yoga, sunlight, and meditation are examples of types of remedies if your problems are rooted here. These practices keep the physical body vital and protected from the negative astral beings that slip into the Ethereal Realm. When negative astral beings slide into the Ethereal Realm, they will attempt to jump into the ethereal body of a person with a weak ethereal body. When the negative being is firmly rooted in the ethereal body, the hijacked person will feel abnormal energy levels in the body. The traits of this negative being will start to manifest in the physical body as actual physical symptoms. Sexual excess, lack of sleep, overwork, anxiety, unresolved emotional trauma, and a lack of energetically charged foods can cause wormholes for this type of negative astral hijacking and those beings that bring sleep paralysis.

Spirits: *The realm of your spiritual double, sleep paralysis beings, passive nature qi*

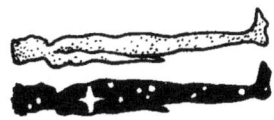

REALM 4, THE ASTRAL REALM

Realm 4, the **Astral Realm**, is the realm of water and dreams. The waters are the original element and energetic foundation of all, as reflected physically by our oceans. Every night we return to the waters in this subconscious realm of dreams, and timelessness. All beings are free to move in this space of limitless emotional and creative potential that houses the bodies we use to travel through our emotions and high subtle realms. When we sleep, we are gathering this charged spiritual water into our ethereal cups (rooted in the Ethereal Realm) to gather astral waters to fuel our bodies for the next day. Dream journaling, extremely emotional ceremonies, talking from the heart with people, walking into a body of water, or facing your shadow side—all are ways of moving through this realm. This realm is no respecter of time or fact. A fictional person is just as "real" as a living person in this realm, and they can both learn from each other. This is not a space of differentiation between fake and real. This is a space of dreams and limitless fluid communication. It's a ground zero where anything is possible. I could just as easily talk to Malcolm X as I could speak to my future self in this space. This realm can take on a more linear usage when paired with the Mental Realm. When the Astral Realm is linked with the Mental Realm, dream interpretation becomes a priority and dreams become lucid. When the Astral Realm is linked with the Intuitive Realm, the "dream" then spills outward into supernatural waking experiences such as gaining the ability to project the astral body outside of the Astral Realm. Astral travel links the Astral Realm to the Mental Realm and the Intuitive Realm. These three realms also open up access to past lives, and an ability to see spirits unseen to most through third eye and heart-linked vision.

Spirits: *Ghosts, subconscious and dreamed beings, astral beings*

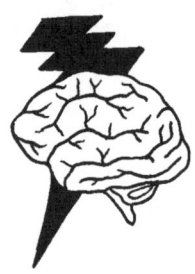

REALM 5, THE MENTAL REALM

Realm 5, the **Mental Realm**, is the realm that governs the gift of the internal planning ground. This realm is the home of the ego and its desire to create and destroy. The Mental Realm is a playground where we can conjure up and plan before we act. It's also a place where we can control symbols and indulge in fantasies and develop the focus necessary to find peace or the best way to carry out tasks. Finding a therapist or a life coach could be a great way to find balance in this plane. It could also help to read various authors or do some writing about your daily mental state. This is the realm of your personal willpower. It is the realm of "mind over matter." You have to use your mind to push through. The Mental Realm plays with, takes apart, pieces together, and interacts with anything introduced to it from any of the other realms. When you are introduced to someone, you build another version of them in your mind's eye. They do the same. This can become dangerous if someone starts wishing evil upon the version of you that they've built in their mind. Every person who is conscious of you sends a cord to you that is activated through their awareness of you existing. It merges with the Intuitive Realm and projects outward as the "evil eye."

This is the realm where story medicine is strongest. The effects of story medicine are often called the "placebo effect." There are energies in our subconscious that rely on certain types of attention and stories in order to flourish. If that subconscious need is not being met, the person might become depressed or even get physically ill. A medicine or task or object with the right life-giving story attached to it can recharge the subconscious energies, and the person's symptoms will disappear. Sometimes this story medicine needs to be given by a healer full of mysteries and wisdom; and other types of story medicine can be given to the self through reciting positive affirmations, praying, reading, watching movies, or meditating. Sometimes requests from a healer can sound foolish because they are speaking to your subconscious. A healer could say, "You must get your old flute and go outside right before sunrise. Play that old flute with all your heart so the sun will rise. You'll feel better." This would sound awfully foolish to the Western rational thinker who knows the sun will rise no matter what. What the healer knows is that there are many suns, and they must be aligned. The healing sun within your heart may be stuck in the underworld. Playing a heartfelt flute for the physical sun could link the two suns. This could lead to a clearing up of symptoms linked to your own inner sun and its entrapment.

Spirits: *Thoughtforms, memory loops, and imagined beings*

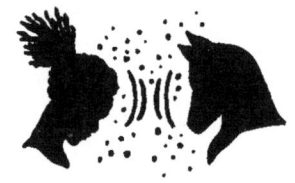

REALM 6, THE INTUITIVE REALM

Realm 6, the **Intuitive Realm**, is the super psychic realm that links all light bodies. It usually manifests in our lives as a way of telepathic communication that happens during our waking states. Its matrix allows a form of communication without the use of sound that is also accessible over long physical distances.

Human beings can use intuitive senses more or less, depending upon the level of natural talent versus the years of intuitive or psychic development. The intuitive senses can be consciously projected with the use of willful powers of the mind. When the mental powers are blended with the emotional Astral Realm, it's often called *imagination*. When the mental powers are blended with the intuition, this is called psychic communication. The energy produced through the merging of realms that create imagination can over time lead to full conscious activation of the Intuitive Realm. The Intuitive Realm is like a web with various strands building communication connectivity between places, people, and beings. There are higher beings in Realms 7 and above always tugging, activating, and tying these lines from you to other people, places, and beings as well. These often manifest as what appears to be a random notion to call someone, move from a place, and so on. As you build your relationship with intuition, just remember that it starts with imagining the connections you wish to make. Over time, this will develop into a solid psychic connection. Before you know it, you'll be able to consciously project the light of your intuitive body deep into a tree or an animal or even across seas to a friend. This light will hit the intuitive body of the target and you'll gain information, not controlled by your own will, that can't be obtained directly from other realms alone.

The Intuitive Realm is like the Ethereal Realm and the Astral Realm in that it is highly receptive to crystals and stones. To absorb energy, it is wise to place the crystals or stones upon the left wrist. If the left wrist is receiving so much crystal energy that it becomes uncomfortable, remove any bracelet or change it to the right wrist. Some crystals need to be on the left wrist for only a short time. If the cards or some other medium tell you that your issues are rooted here in this realm, find the correct stones, start meditating in natural surroundings, or visualize a light around you and start powering up often.

Spirits: *Telepathic currents, holy guardian angel, nature spirits, totem beings and light beings, light senses*

REALM 7, THE ANCESTRAL REALM

Realm 7, the **Ancestral Realm,** is the realm of collective bodies of bloodlinked clans and their foods, dances, and cultures. If this type of card is the primary focus, it's important to ask yourself about the theme of your lineage. How are your folks doing in the afterlife? Do they leave any signs for you? What gifts and curses have been passed down? What medicines were granted to you? What medicine do you bring to the legacy of your bloodline? What names for God or Spirit have your people relied upon? We can call whatever deities are interested in us, but the spirits that answer first are in the *blood*! What oral traditions have been passed down? What prayers did you find in Granny's journal? For how many generations did your ancestors sing spirit-filled gospel to a soulful Christ figure? That music is in the *blood*! Do you have any records or hunches that your ancestors honored other traditions? Are you visited by beings in dreams or visions that mention names such as Yemaya, Agwe, Eshu, or Obatala? Those would be callings to ancestral ways and the spirits that correspond to them. The energy is still available because the blood remembers how to utilize those frequencies. This ancestral energy potential in the blood is accessible only as the rituals and ways that summon them. This is one of the reasons that rites of passage are so important. Some of us have illness or stagnancy within our lives because of a ritual or ancestral rites of passage that our blood needs to activate certain ancestral strengths. This is why learning who you are and who you were is so important! You are a member of a large collective ancestral body that has needs.

The rays of life bounce off this collective ancestral body to determine how you receive subtle energies before they land upon the spirit of your mind. Rhythms and culture and foods can affect people differently based on this wave. If you are having problems in this plane, it's also important to make an offering to your ancestors, show grace to your family/clan, and/or activate the ancestors within by learning a cultural dance, singing, working with plants or power animals, or playing the music that has always fed your bloodline. It could also be beneficial to fully initiate into an ancestral tradition. It is important to note that when working with ancestors, we differentiate the word "ancestor" from "dead relative." When we call upon ancestors, we are calling upon those within the bloodline who were healed enough to walk in a good way. It is wise to call in ancestors. Ancestor is an earned title from a life well lived. Random "dead relatives" should not be called upon. Instead, call upon your enlightened ancestors known and unknown while also working with people who you had a great personal relationship with while they lived on Earth.

When the Ancestral Realm is accessed through the Intuitive Realm, it could induce trancelike states or even a downloading of special ancestral skills.

Spirits: *Ancestors, bloodlinked clans*

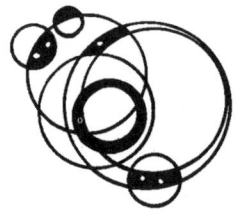

REALM 8, THE COINCIDENCE REALM

Realm 8, the **Coincidence Realm,** is the realm of synchronicity, curses, and good luck. If this realm is sick in your spirit, you will experience many setbacks. Timing will always be working against you, and things will always seem to break down around you no matter what. Divination and astrological readings are great ways to diagnose the details of what is going on here. This is a realm of action and your overall story potentials, so it is important to place yourself in the right story that strengthens your spirits. Let your forces help you by being in the right spaces! It is also important to untie any cords from relationships to spaces, spells, or people that are no longer reciprocal.

Spirits: Astrological influences, planetary influences, coincidence bodies, divination

REALM 9, THE MYTHIC REALM

Realm 9, the **Mythic Realm**, is the home of potent symbols and potencies of power that activate and call in strong forces, lost technology of star people, and all saints and mysterious powerful entities. If your problems are rooted in this plane, you want to summon or send prayers to your most proven and powerful spirits. Some would even call this the realm of the Most High Beings or even the Throne of God, Allah, or Olodumare. If you pull a card that corresponds to this realm, it could be telling you to use your best mantras, power symbols, or big plant medicines to go into the deep. Miracles aren't usually far from this realm.

Spirits: God, gods, saints, orishas, Reiki energy

Ways to Balance Each Realm

Listed below are offerings or ways to honor the needs that a particular realm asks for.

Realm 1. **Nighttime** **Object Realm**	add, feed, or take away spiritual objects from the altar or home
Realm 2. **Physical Realm**	dense nutritious foods, proper medications, exercise and fasting
Realm 3. **Ethereal Realm**	breathing techniques, yoga, prana-rich foods, flower essences for the body
Realm 4. **Astral Realm**	recording dreams, astral traveling, bonding, crying, expressing emotion, music, art
Realm 5. **Mental Realm**	developing focus, reading, willpower, visualization, counseling, compartmentalizing, studying, habits
Realm 6. **Intuitive Realm**	going into nature and connecting, channeling, altar work, going within for answers, practices that develop and maintain the inner world
Realm 7. **Ancestral Realm**	ancestral ceremony, marriage, initiation, rites of passage, prayers, songs, foods, and ways of dress passed down the lineage; honoring and drawing in support of the ancestors

Realm 8. Coincidence Realm	cutting or changing friend groups or places, going to a diviner or looking at astrological charts, numerology or magic that brings good luck and changes the outer world to fit needs and probabilties
Realm 9. Mythic Realm	being charged with ancient sounds and symbols, visiting powerful or mysterious holy cities, mystery schools

HERBAL HEALING DIAGNOSTICS

This oracle deck is designed to guide someone who loves plant medicines and shamanic-based practices in how to look clearly at the source of a problem and its specific plant remedies. Once someone begins to practice with the deck, they automatically become a reader. This reader is the interpreter for their very own healing, and so every reader is a healer.

An important reality of the Walking Tree Oracle is the fact that we are living in a multidimensional world. Everything in existence also exists in multiple realms at once. Parts of our complete being, as well as illnesses in all their forms, are not exempt from this multidimensional reality. Illness doesn't come only from microbes and viruses; it can come from emotional blockages, mental sludge, and even generational curses.

As stated, each card contains a symbol that links the reader's inquiry to one of the primary nine realms mentioned above.

If the reader is having an issue with stomach pain, the reader can shuffle the deck with that specific issue in mind and draw a card. The card pulled will be linked to one of the nine realms. It will tell the reader where to prioritize their focus. This nine-realms model is the backbone of the deck. Each realm corresponds to the energetic layer of a human, ranging all the way from the physical body to the more subtle bodies. The card pulled indicates a specific realm, ritual, and way to use herbs to be rid of the problem. The card tells which realm is the true carrier of the root of the problem you are facing. This is important because symptoms can often appear in a realm separate from the root cause.

If the card pulled is linked to Realm 2, for example, the reader knows that the root of the problem lies deep in the physical body. Once the reader knows that the problem lies deep in the physical body, the reader can focus on plant chemicals or some other purely physical medium to hit the core issue behind the stomach pain. On the other hand, if the reader chooses a card linked to the emotional Realm 4, that would indicate a much deeper emotional root. The reader would not find relief from mere chemicals and minerals in this case. They would need to acknowledge that the pain is rooted in unresolved emotional energies that must be focused upon.

RITUALS AND HERBS FOR HEALING

Aside from learning the root dimension holding the illness, there are two other benefits for the reader. First, the card and associated realm will also have a ritual mentioned in the book. The reader (who is, by definition, anyone using this deck) would be able to read the ritual that pertains to the card and repeat the ritual as a spiritual medicine to aid them through the healing process. Second is the herbal aspect to this deck. The medicinal herbs and various plant spirits that correspond to the selected realm are mentioned in the book as allies. The reader who drew the Realm 4 card in regard to their stomachache can read the Realm 4 section of the book and find these special plant allies and exactly which way to use them (smudge, tea, or altar work).

Realm Herbal Affinities

Realm	Plants	How to Use
1. Nighttime Object/ Artifact	juniper branches, elder branches, yellow dock root, ginkgo (branches are strongest in Spring and Roots strong in Autumn)	Branches must still have leaves attached as you hang them in the home, or place fresh roots by the bedside. If roots are dried, speak your intention upon them and/or anoint them with oil.

Realm	Plants	How to Use
2. Physical	echinacea, ashwagandha, dandelion, red raspberry leaves	Brewing herbal tea will suffice. The plant chemicals do all the work here. Pay close attention, and feel the spirit of those plant constituents move in the body.
3. Ethereal	garlic, basil	Add these food herbs to your diet in higher amounts and be sure to move in sunlight and/or do a few yoga poses daily.
4. Astral	mugwort, rose, kava	Mugwort tea before bed with dream journal, kava as tea, or rose facial spray.
5. Mental	ginkgo, rosemary, gotu kola	Add infused oils or essential oils to temples. Also consume as tincture or tea.
6. Intuitive	St. John's wort, lavender, sage, artemisia	Smudge home with artemisia or sage, lavender pillow, meditation: see a golden light, a golden light coming from St. John's wort flowers and see the light move all around you for protection.

Realm	Plants	How to Use
7. Ancestral	marigolds, tobacco	Blow tobacco smoke upon the altar or lay fresh marigold upon the altar.
8. Coincidence	rue, basil	Wash walls and floor with infusion made of rue. Spray vehicle with basil or wear basil leaf in pocket or pouch for good luck. Place rue under tongue for power over situation.
9. Mythic	copal, frank-incense, myrrh	Smudge and meditate or pray your heart's desire at least weekly.

Additionally, a plant spirit is associated with all of the Major Arcana cards. So if the reader wants to ask who their spirit guide is or which plant to place upon an altar, all they have to do is ask, shuffle, and choose a card. They'll find the plant that corresponds to that card in the book.

ZODIAC CORRESPONDENCE: DETERMINING THE DISEASE MODALITY

Once the disease is located, the modality of the disease can also be identified through the deck based on the zodiac sign with which it is associated. There are *fixed* signs, *cardinal* signs, and *mutable* signs. A fixed disease is chronic, meaning that it's extremely slow-moving, is harder to remove without exact keys, and tends to pop back up from time to time even if you thought it was cured. Cardinal diseases are usually acute and seasonal. They hit hard and can quickly be gone as if they were never there. Mutable diseases don't lock on very tightly to their prey. They can usually be kicked without needing to be too specific in how you fight them. If you wish to know the nature of a disease, draw the card and check out the zodiac sign associated with it.

Modality	Description	Signs
Fixed	has to go through a process and can't usually be removed all the way in an instant. It can only be eased through its process. It can appear to be gone while it sleeps.	Leo, Scorpio, Taurus, Aquarius
Cardinal	hits hard and fast and must be knocked out with exact, pinpointed precision	Aries, Cancer, Capricorn, Libra
Mutable	fickle, unstable, and easy to remove with a broad stroke	Sagittarius, Pisces, Virgo, Gemini

PLANETARY CORRESPONDENCE: THE NATURE OF THE DISEASE AND HERBAL AFFINITIES

Each oracle card also corresponds to a specific planet. Each planet can give major clues into the nature of a disease and which types of herbs a person may want to take internally, wear, or place on an altar based on the planet and realm affected.

Sun	warm and energizing
Moon	cool and wet; the inner nature
Mercury	tight and nervous
Venus	relaxed, wet, nourishing and soothing
Mars	forceful, hot, energized, irritated or inflamed
Jupiter	warm, damp, and expansive
Saturn	dry, cold, hard, and restrictive
Uranus	sudden, electric, and nervous
Neptune	dissolving, mysterious; sometimes poisonous or toxic
Pluto	generational, transformative, deep

Planetary Herbal Affinities

Solar Plants

Solar plants are extra reactive to the sun and prefer areas that get much of it. Their solar power can also appear solar in how they ray out. Many in this group have the actual ray flowers. Yellow and orange are also common colors. The solar power manifesting through these plants can generally add warmth to the body, often working through the pungent taste. The solar plants remove stagnation and begin to make the blood circulate much better, which increases nutrient absorption in the gut. These plants may induce sweating as they push energy up and out. They increase heat to the body and aid with cold, damp conditions. **Plants**: *echinacea, sunflowers, and yarrow*

Lunar Plants

Moon plants often love swampy, boggy conditions and can have a silvery or whitish look to them. Moon plants are sweet or bland with a mucilaginous or demulcent action. Flowers can be blue or purple. Some of the lunar qualities can manifest as sleep-inducing and/or hypnotic. Melons grow close to the earth, in the same way the moon has the largest and most immediate effect on the Earth. Moon plants strengthen those who need hydration and moisture and coolness. Moon plants work on breastmilk production, can help move the lymph, and help with fluid regulation in general. **Plants**: *mugwort, other artemisias such as sagebrush, and watermelon*

Mercurial Plants

Mercurial plants have both hollow and square stems and appear bronchial in nature. They are amazing communicators and therefore have much to say aromatically. They tend to be great tonics for the lungs and help the release of gas trapped in the gut. Mercury pushes a mind toward focus and can also help modulate nervous activity. Mercury manifests strongly within the entire mint family. **Plants**: *mint, gotu kola, lobelia, and ginkgo*

Venusian Plants

Venusian plants are often five petaled and pink or yellow in color. They tend to be showy and delicate looking. Venusian plants can also taste and smell like a perfume, because of the Venusian appreciation for cleanliness. Damiana has a perfumy smell and is also astringent to tone skin, aiding in the Venus specialty. Yarrow can be perfumy as well and has extremely soft fernlike leaves, which is also said to be Venusian. Venus brings in romantic energy that comes with relaxation. Venusian plants can also be somewhat nervine and antispasmodic. **Plants**: *damiana, roses, and linden*

Martian Plants

Martian plants are often red, or prickly, or extremely hot and spicy. Inside or out, they will make it a point to show their intensity somewhere. These plants bring blood and heat to the extremities through aiding the circulation. They are said to leave a tingling sensation on the tongue at times. Stimulants like coffee are also governed by Mars.

Cayenne pepper is a stimulant for the blood/circulation that raises core body heat and relieves excess internal heat. Mars is also reflected in a rejuvenating tonic to bring back vitality, testicular power, and testosterone-driven masculine power. **Plants**: *onions (intense heat, ears in the eyes), nettle (prickly to skin), cayenne (intense to mouth and skin), prickly ash, coffee*

Jovian Plants

Jovian plants often like to spread out with big, broad leaves. Flowers can often be yellow, which is one of the old ways of recognizing Jupiter plants. Sometimes the root can inspire the holding of water (licorice). This was said to be due to a connection between Jupiter and the bile. Bile is formed in the liver, which is the great organizer of the body. Many of the Jovian plants aid the liver, creating cleansing for a damp, stagnant condition. Fruits from Jupiter plants are often thick and oily. **Plants**: *avocado, burdock, and potatoes*

Saturnian Plants

Saturnian plants are strong and fibrous and tough. They are full of minerals that aid the body. They can sometimes be knobby as though they have knees. Saturn governs the knees and the bones. Saturn is said to have a somewhat spooky type of energy because of the planet's association with death. Saturnian plants are usually bitter and draining. You'll often feel hungry after drinking these teas. Saturnian plants are great for toxic, damp conditions and folks that are overly hot. ***Plants***: *comfrey (toxic internally), boneset, horsetail*

Uranian Plants

Uranian plants either are strong nervines or are utilized in accordance with the technology of the age. As soon as a plant has been broken down by humans and used in a new (and potentially dangerous) way, it belongs to Uranus. Homeopathics belong to Uranus as well. Super strong nervines also go into this section, because Uranus is extremely strong and extremely electric. ***Plants***: *anemone, pedicularis, Jamaican dogwood, Mercurial plants*

Neptunian Plants

Most Neptunian plants grow underwater, float on water, or work in mysterious ways that can't always be linked to measurable constituents. Neptunian plants have a high affinity to the pineal gland as well. Kelp, which grows in saltwater, and also the freshwater spirulina fall into this class of plants. The water-loving lotus plants also belong in this class of herbs. This includes the famous blue lotus, whose mysterious properties were celebrated throughout ancient Egypt. ***Plants***: *kelp, spirulina, blue lotus, yellow pond lily, dream herb, and Moon plants such as mugwort*

Plutonian Plants

Plutonian plants are the most mysterious of all. They carry the weight to fight off curses that exist through lineages. Plants in this category are typically used by various cultures as ancestral medicines. ***Plants****: impepho tea or smudge, helichrysum essential oil, strong ceremonial plants*

FAITH AND HERBS

Faith and herbs come together to make extremely powerful medicine! This is an important thing to know because faith or a sure belief in some type of healing is an opener for other medicinal forces tied to the plant spirit. Think of faith as a muscle that opens the spiritual mouth so that subtle medicines can flow in. If we want our medicines to "work," we must also understand the difference between "desired result" and "work." If a plant medicine doesn't give you the desired result, that doesn't mean it didn't work. Work is an action, felt or unfelt, that the plant has done for you. Even if you can't feel it, that plant medicine did some work for you. That is why we must have faith and also respect, whether or not we reach the desired result. Plants do not all work on the same dimension or in the same way. For example, you may pray and take plant medicine for headaches. Let's say the headache doesn't go away because the plant chose not to work physically. Instead, the plant spirit decides to place most of its energy toward Realm 8, the Coincidence Realm. The plant spirit as a guide helps you to bump into a friend who wants you to go on a sugar fast with her. You do the sugar fast and the headache goes away. This is how deeply and mysteriously your plant medicines can work for you. If you do not get your desired result, you shouldn't go around saying it didn't work. You don't want the plant spirit to ever stop working for you. Instead, it is wiser to say that you didn't get the desired result and will try another plant to reach it. It is powerful and very respectful to the plant spirit to chant, "My medicines always work!"

Speaking of respect, it is also important to note that in this paradigm, placebo does not exist. If you do get the desired result, do not go around saying you don't know if it was really the medicine that healed you. Always give credit to the plant spirit and say, "Thank you." There is no true placebo, as most of us think of it. Many people think of a placebo as "fake medicine." No, a better name for this type of medicine is "story medicine." If the root cause of a physical illness is in Realm 5, the Mental Realm, then a proper story will have proper physical results. If I tie a healing story to a sugar pill, claiming that it is a cure for a sore throat, that sore throat will instantly start to feel better if the root cause is in Realm 5, the Mental Realm. If the root is in another realm, the story will still help, but in a subtle way, as everything has some mental energy attached. For example, if someone is bleeding to death, which is an emergency rooted in the Physical Realm, mental story medicine will not suffice in treatment.

THE MIND AND THE POWER OF CEREMONY

In this section we look at ways that this oracle deck can be used as a ritual tool to help guide and create sacred space—in your environment and in your own heart. You'll be able to banish and bless spaces using tree branches, roots, and the oracle deck together. A regular practice can shift our relationships with our immediate environment and reinforce powerful portals for working with our guides and spirit helpers.

MIND MEDICINE (WHAT KIND OF DREAM ARE YOU IN?)

Concepts	
Archetype Mind	the deep and unchangeable mental landscape
Mid-Conscious	the changeable part of the subconscious mind that projects through the eyes to create unconscious perception
Conscious Mind	the mind we are aware of in a waking state; also known as the Waking Mind
FLOWER	a highly charged healing thought-form in the Mid-Conscious

WEED	a highly charged trouble-causing thoughtform in the Mid-Conscious
PLANT	a FLOWER or a WEED in the Mid-Conscious
SEED	a potential PLANT (FLOWER or WEED) in the Mid-Conscious
LIGHT	a strong dream that shines through the eyes to project a reality into the Conscious Mind

The human mind is made of three parts that all work together to determine behavior, perception of reality, and how challenges are processed: the Archetype Mind, the Mid-Conscious, and the Conscious Mind. The Archetype Mind and the Mid-Conscious are both parts of the mind we can't usually access directly. They are both aspects of what we might know as the "subconscious."

The **Archetype Mind**, or deep subconscious, is the part of us that is linked to archetypes. These archetypes are living stories and themes that form the blueprint for the type of mind any person can have. For example, if one of your archetypes is The Martyr, that archetype would always work hard to make sure that your mind is tempered and shaped in a way that makes you aware of sacrificial martyr themes and understandings in this life. Through learning, shadow work, spiritual living, and divination, the goal is to work with your archetypes in ways that are healthy. These archetypes, which are a culmination of our astrological paths, power animals, places of birth, and ancestry, work together through us, mingling in various ways to create our potential life paths via our inner landscape called the mind. We are born with these archetypes in place and will always be feeding and energizing them throughout our life choices.

One key note on the Archetype Mind is that it can't be altered or changed in any way. Our life themes or archetypes are pre-set and fixed based on pre-life agreements and hard contracts. The archetypes are the internal ecosystem, the foundational and magnetic soils, as well as the weather patterns of your mind. For you, the farmer, it's important to build a proper home for that environment and discard any PLANTS growing in your internal garden that may prove poisonous or nonbeneficial. I often picture the archetypes as a group of gods weaving their threads together to create the foundational quilt that we will both live and dream upon.

The **Mid-Conscious**, or superficial subconscious, is the vast mental/emotional internal garden or "auto-pilot plane." It tends to be easily recognizable by what is done without consciously thinking. For example, many of us make decisions first and then make up reasons as to why we did it. The illusion of choice was there, but there was really no true choice, because the road was already picked in the Mid-Conscious. The Mid-Conscious is built on top of the archetypical terrain mixed with patches of troubling WEEDS and patches of beautiful FLOWERS. I capitalize these words to differentiate them from their regular use.

WEEDS and FLOWERS grow in our inner landscape in the same way that plants grow in soil. WEEDS and FLOWERS are also very similar to each other in that they begin as seeds in your inner landscape that need energy and nourishment in order to grow. They then establish a root system that absorbs nutrients from the inner landscape while also energizing a particular archetype. When WEEDS and FLOWERS come to full maturity, they give off a brilliant LIGHT that brightens the inner landscape. This LIGHT reveals a part of the inner landscape in a particular way and creates a reality that projects onto the outer world of the individual.

This is how we dream while we are awake. We never see an objective reality. Instead, what we are perceiving is seen only through the LIGHT given off by a WEED or FLOWER in the Mid-Conscious. This is why different people can see the same exact thing in a different way. They can see based only on the available LIGHTS or "light paths" they have. WEEDS project LIGHTS that feed our inner archetypes in ways that work against our evolution.

Partaking in actions that are the result of LIGHT that is emanated by WEEDS drains life force, distracts from deeper soul missions, and can sometimes just be down-right dangerous.

FLOWERS in the Mid-Conscious project LIGHTS that feed our inner archetypes in ways that feed our deep-est potentials for evolution. Moving in ways that are the result of FLOWER LIGHT increases life force over time and pulls us closer to our deepest soul missions. These LIGHTS are a major foundation for our inner resonance and what we will base our waking rational thought upon. Actions based on the strongest LIGHTS you emit will seem most logical.

There are many LIGHTS emanating from within us, some even handed down from past lives or dead relatives, but the dominant LIGHT will always get the energy it wants; and its projections will be reinforced by strong emotions and thoughtforms until its death. LIGHTS are how we move when we are on auto-pilot. Therefore, the things we assume without much thought are LIGHTS. It's key to know that whatever we don't know about our world is filled in for us by our LIGHTS.

We often build our logical deductions based on those LIGHTS first. In other words, we are consciously walk-ing on the LIGHTS grown in our own Mid-Conscious gardens.

The **Conscious Mind** uses logic and strategy to con-sciously move through the projected emotions, reso-nances, and realities projecting outward from within. This

Conscious Mind is our Waking Mind that works so hard to make rational sense of it all so that we can be productive members of society and/or feel good about ourselves. This fact has worked against Black folks and all oppressed people around the world. There is a huge LIGHT that spawns from a WEED called white supremacy. It is radiated into our inner landscapes through our schooling, parental upbringing, media, songs, and spoken languages, to name a few of its forms. This radiation enters into our minds like a toxic rainstorm and feeds our inner SEEDS until they become strong WEEDS that project LIGHTS that allow us to move only in the limited ways that protect the status quo.

The LIGHTS we emanate from within can become extremely strong throughout the years, becoming like trees in our Mid-Conscious. These LIGHTS can be really good for us if they come from FLOWERS; but they can be extremely damaging if they spawn from WEEDS, which can produce only LIGHTS that help maintain magnetism and matrices that keep us from honoring our best lives. It is the LIGHT from the FLOWER that attracts your healers or the people you are able to heal. It is the LIGHT from the WEED that attracts your abusers or those you are destined to abuse with its magnetism. It is the LIGHTS that call in stories that will stalk a person to the ends of the earth just to express their energy. The story clearly sees what you can become based on your LIGHT.

Once that story eats from the energy made through mingling its energy with your own, the satisfying energetic food is sent right to the WEED or FLOWER it came from. This strengthens the PLANT, which then feeds your base archetypes. This is why we must always be careful of being careless or simply reactionary in stories that don't usually end well for us. Moving with ease down a path is good only if it leads to treasure. There are LIGHTS within us that will always attract some things very easily.

Ease does not equal goodness. The more in alignment a story is with an inner LIGHT, the easier things come to you. The ease that comes with strong magnetism feels very intuitive and pleasurable even if it leads to a bad place. This is also what makes infatuation such a dangerous weapon for the feeding of inner WEEDS. A strong infatuation with a person of interest is telling the romance-filled individual only that the person of interest and the story attached to them are in full alignment with a LIGHT. This LIGHT could be a LIGHT from a WEED or a FLOWER. If every time a person falls in love they get burned in the same way, it's time to stop falling in love. This is because that person is only falling into stories emitted by WEEDS. No matter how pleasant that attraction feels, the red flags must be noticed. There are general red flags, but there are also very personal red flags that you know through living out the same story over and over again. Once a person learns from falling into the WEEDS enough times, they can end the era of falling in love and instead begin to stand in awareness.

Some WEEDS can be pulled out completely. Others, usually the ones inherited through severe trauma or generational trauma, can take many years or even a lifetime to even weaken. Much of these will require additional assistance from an experienced teacher or mentor or spiritual group. A deeper truth is that we can even use the LIGHT from WEEDS to our advantage. I know people who have fallen into the same WEED patterns for so long that they can immediately recognize a bad character or story before the evils attached to them begin to emerge. Sometimes the best option is even just to stay away from places where those monstrous stories exist. I know people who used to fight at bars and nightclubs but never fight anymore because they simply don't go to bars and nightclubs. They learned from the WEED. This learning from a WEED weakens its influence and instead strengthens a SEED that will become a FLOWER to make a LIGHT that attracts a new story.

LIGHTS from PLANTS (WEEDS or FLOWERS) can become extremely strong. All LIGHTS are not created equal. LIGHTS can get so strong that they can combine and create a solid group LIGHT. These group LIGHTS are like strong trees that can fill the soul of anyone susceptible. Diversity is important so that one group

LIGHT doesn't dominate the minds of the entire globe. LIGHTS and group LIGHTS offer us many different ways to see the world and experience the stories we attract individually and collectively. Even in death, our LIGHTS crystallize into a consciousness that can be accessed and drawn from. In some cultures, these crystallized LIGHTS can be handed down from one shaman to another through various objects, prayers, and charged gestures.

I imagine that people who lived and died, becoming saints or orishas, have very strong LIGHTS spinning upon various planes inspiring millions of people every day. This crystalline LIGHT shell is a part of you that will still be accessible even after your soul goes into another timeline to reincarnate.

Your thoughts and emotions will fight like heck in order to protect the strongest LIGHTS that you emit. So it is necessary to develop patience and the reflective sides of self so we can be honest with what those LIGHTS bring to us. Through this work, you may realize that some of your strongest LIGHTS (that often come with immediate reactions and assumptions) are just distorted LIGHT from something truly alien to where your spirit really wants to be.

The Walking Tree Oracle is a system that is provided as a tool that we can use along with dreams and other systems to look into the Mid-Conscious and get a good look at what is happening in there.

My prayer is that we all work with our WEEDS and FLOWERS in a way that helps us to create many amazing cultural expressions of harmonious individual and group LIGHTS that anchor us with the LIGHT radiating from the mind of nature and its nine dimensional truths. May the minds of humans not rely upon LIGHTS that are like artificial trees with human hearts clinging to them. I would like to see a world where the LIGHTS of humans fuse with the LIGHT of the natural environment and the heart of the forest in a way that produces balance and abundance for all harmonious and natural creatures seen and unseen.

The Walking Tree Oracle deck can help us to bring all three parts of our world together in a way that leads to our greatest self-expression. Here's how to do it:

The Mind Unity Spread

Shuffle the deck while thinking or speaking about your situation, and separate the deck into three stacks. Pull one card from the first stack. This card is the main archetype you are feeding through your particular situation. Pull two cards from the middle stack and set them side by side. The one to the left represents the WEED that is hurting the situation, and the one to the right represents the FLOWER that we want to strengthen.

From the last stack, pull a card to represent the types of actions you must consciously take to weaken the WEED and strengthen the FLOWER. We'll call this card the "remedy card." If you pull a Royal Court card, this represents a person that you have a relationship with who can aid in your success. Pull another card, which will show you exactly **how** you both will work together to attain the best result.

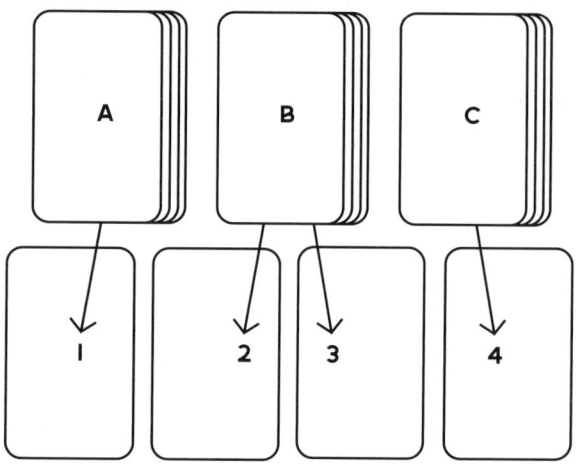

Advanced: Core Mind Unity Spread

NOTE The Core Mind Unity Spread is intended as a spread to be used only once in order to read the three core unchanging archetypes in a person. This reading is very important. A picture should be taken, and notes should be written. This reading follows a person for a lifetime, adding important information on the gifts and struggles of this incarnation.

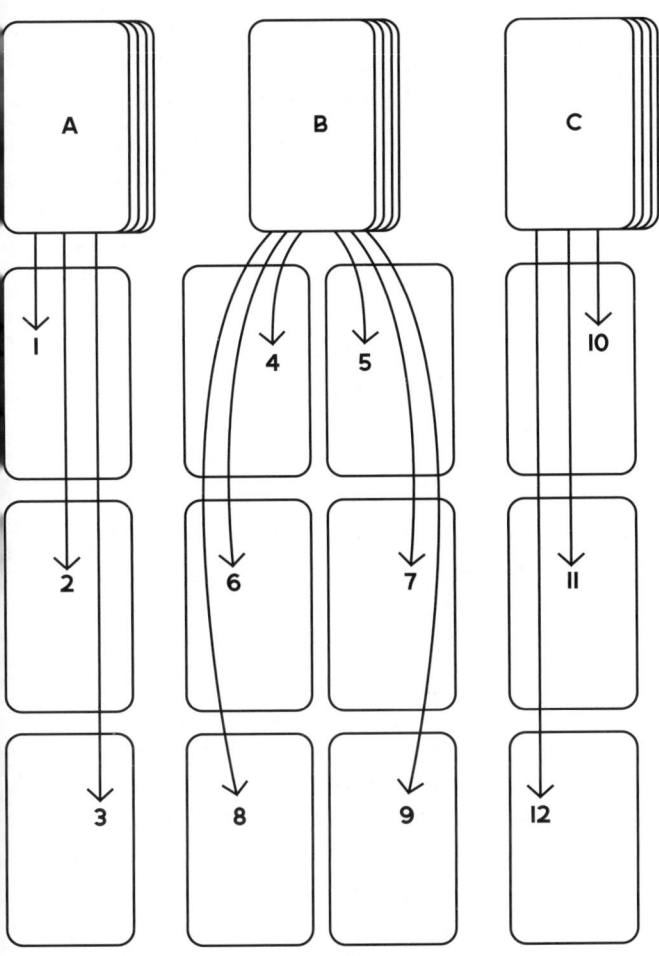

Shuffle the deck while thinking or speaking about your situation, and separate into three stacks. Pull three cards in a straight line from the first stack. These three cards are the main archetypes you are feeding through your existence. Pull six cards from the middle stack in the following way: Pull one to the left to represent the WEED and one to the right to represent the FLOWER until you get three pairs.

From the last stack, pull three cards to represent the types of actions you must consciously take to weaken the WEED and strengthen the FLOWER in the pair that wishes to influentially take its place. We'll call this last row of cards pulled the "remedy cards." If you pull a Royal Court card, this represents a person that you have a relationship with who can aid in your success. Pull another card, which will show you exactly **how** you both will work together to attain the best result.

The Nine-Day Ritual Spread

This spread is for a quick look into the mind for a specific issue. For example, if you have fears or anxieties that pop up when you enter certain spaces due to trauma or reasons not understood, this spread is for you.

Shuffle the deck with your question in mind. Place the deck down and pick three cards. Place them in front of you from left to right. Flip the first card to see which archetype is at the root of your issue. Now flip the second card. The second card represents the fear- or anxiety-causing WEED growing within the inner landscape. Now flip the third card. The third card represents the ritual and the energies you must implement in your waking reality in order to combat the WEED that is radiating its stifling LIGHT into your reality. Complete the rituals mentioned by this card in rotations of nine consecutive days until your goal is reached.

NOTE PLANTS (WEEDS and FLOWERS) require water to live. When we are processing through a particular PLANT, some of its water will be released through our tears. When we weep in bitterness, jealousy, insincerity, or self-serving anger, or are trying to control other sovereign beings, we are watering a WEED. When we weep in joy rooted in deep gratitude and humility, sincerely weep for the pain of another, or weep through a season of emotional growth and learning, we are watering a FLOWER. When the waters dry up, or there is no emotion, the PLANT is dried up. Another PLANT may take over and produce a different behavior or emotion.

A Step Further: Getting to the Mid-Conscious
Now that we know our WEEDS and our FLOWERS, which cards are associated with them, and the cards associated with our liberation from those WEEDS, it's time to step things up a bit. What if we could use ceremony to create a portal into our Mid-Conscious to pull out some WEEDS? Well …! That's exactly what we are going to do!

After you perform the Mind Unity Spread, leave the spread out and perform The Four Directions Prayer (see below). Light some sage or blow out some tobacco. Pour some water upon the earth or in a glass and say, "Blessed Water, Blessed Paths, Blessed Shelters, Blessed Clothing, Blessed Foods, Blessed Air, Blessed Guardian Angels, Blessed Ancestors, Blessed Guides. I release the WEEDS bound to me. I ask that they be cut!" Pick up the top card from the last row of the Mind Unity Spread and do a cutting motion right above the WEED card while outwardly praying against it. Do the same thing for all the WEED cards while using the remedy card in its row.

FUN NOTE Fairies and other mischievous beings love to work on the Mid-Conscious directly, which makes them such good tricksters. This is one reason why it's always good to be respectful in nature, so that you don't hide your car keys from yourself!

RITUAL AND PRAYERS

Ritual Space Setup for This Oracle Deck

When working seriously with this deck, set up an altar containing a few special objects to represent each of the nine realms:

1. A thick plant root or tree leaves to represent the underworld, or Nighttime Object Realm

2. A silver dollar or a stone to represent the Physical Realm

3. A candle to represent the movement of qi throughout the Ethereal Realm

4. Water to represent the emotional Astral Realm

5. Smudge or burning incense to represent the Mental Realm

6. An egg or quartz to represent the Intuitive Realm

7. A small holy book, a sacred statue, or a picture of ancestors to represent the Ancestral Realm

8. Dice or a small box of playing cards to represent the Coincidence Realm

9. An ankh, a cross, a secret name of God, or another sacred symbol to represent the Mythic Realm

The Prayer to Filter Unwanted Beings

Before you start pulling cards, definitely make sure that your spread is being guided by the right beings. Here is an optional protective prayer to activate your altar and serve as added protection before a reading or ceremony.

In the name of my God and my ancestors,
And by the power of Apeamiacm, the nine realms,
I call in all entities that will push me deeper,

only to those paths that will bring me to a future
that reflects my most joyous, loved, successful, and
purpose-filled outcomes.

May this oracle bend all time-space,
that all my potential selves may conspire against any igno-
rance or unhealed wounds that I move with today.

May the stories and reflections that come with each
future step also color my past,
so that even when I remember the worst of times, I
only see lessons learned, a ministry for the suffering,
and become filled with peace.

May this deck, and the sacred technology it holds, be a
blessing to me every time I tap into its mysteries.

Asé

The Four Directions Prayer

If you want to, you can add the previous prayer to this one for added protection. Set a candle on each side of the room or altar.

Light the candle representing the north and say:

I pray to the spirit of the NORTH for
The gift of bones and shrines

The holy books
For foundations of which the earth was seeded
The cool wise energies
The Love of Auset
Truth that is the pattern
The light above, origin, the star people
All the holy lands of earth
The wisdom passed down from elders
The knowers of my oral traditions, both lost and
*   found*
the gnomes and earth elementals, the physical sen-
*   sations, the earth's body of minerals, the Akashic*
*   records, and all righteous kings*
Honoring spirit through stillness

Light the candle representing the south and say:

I pray to the spirit of the SOUTH for
The gift of blood, the animal sacrifice, the meat,
The rum, tobacco and and all offerings building
*   bridges …,*
The trances from dance and song and drum that move
*   the mind so gods can ride me away from traumas in*
*   my mind*
The fire path—
The south is always warmer
Warm Fire
resurrection of Ausar

The magic of the moment
Hearth, heart, and home
The fire
The telepathic language of animals
The joy of the child
The vibrance of the teen
The fire elementals
The righteous queen
Honoring spirit through dance

Light the candle representing the west and say:

I pray to the spirit of the WEST for
The gift of herbs
The mysterious shade of the tree,
The tree branch with the leaves attached
The powerful plant root
The dreams
The water path—west is always wetter
The waters of Nu
The "I know nothing"
The great mystery
Calm waters
The intuited or felt
The aloof and new
The work of the iyami
The The ancestors and newborns

The mermaids and nymphs
The righteous princess

Light the candle representing the east and say:

I pray to the spirit of the EAST for
The gift of prayer
The divinations
The solid proof
The solar path—
The sun that rises in the east
The chariot of Ra
The power of manifestation
The fire spreading air
Cool Air
The clear communication
The crisp air
The full-grown and mature
The light language of man
The path of young adult to full grown
The angels of light
The fairies
The One God
The yang light bodies attached to living beings
The good-natured people
The sharp intellect
The righteous prince

May all four directions work toward my greatest protection

AMEN

YOUR MISSION ON EARTH

PICK A CARD FOR LIFE INCARNATION

NOTE TO THE READER Don't feel locked into the rigid boundaries I've set for this deck. Those boundaries are for the people who need those boundaries. Always feel free to check in with your own intuition by picking the cards you feel drawn to and ask yourself, "What does this say about me and where I wish to go in this life? How can I manifest that reality?" It can also be a fun exercise to choose three cards you feel drawn to or whose meanings you feel drawn to and compare those three with three chosen randomly by destiny, the spirits, or chance!

All of us are born with a full-fledged life mission to accomplish while on the earth plane. We also come into this life with guides who give hints, dreams, and signs from the other side. This deck can help you fully tap into your present life purpose in a few simple steps. Light a candle to the North, pray, and then pour a little water into a cup. Light a candle to the South, pray, and then add water into the cup.

Light a candle to the East, pray, and add more water to the cup. Light a candle to the West, pray, and add the last of the water to the cup. Pick up the Walking Tree Oracle deck and shuffle. Say, "What is the purpose of my birth? Who am I? And what is the main thing I need to watch out for in this lifetime?" Break the deck into three stacks and turn over the top card on each stack.

There are no three cards more important to you than these three cards. Take a picture of them and study them deeply so that you know the rituals and taboos that are associated with these cards. For knowledge about these cards, check the "Cards and Descriptions" section of this book. Cards 22 through 33 are "sacred title" cards that carry sacred roles that must be honored and developed in service to paths 0 through 21, the cards of the traditional Major Arcana.

IN WHICH REALM DO YOUR POWERS LIE?

It is very important for any oppressed people to be reminded about their superpowers. Some folks have an issue with admitting to limitations. The problem isn't seeing your limitations; the problem lies in being bound by them. Some of us have been trained to see our limitations only in ways that empower our enemies. Strengths show you what you truly have to give. Limitations are a blessing, too, because they show you what kind of allies you need. There's power in building community. That is what nature is all about. We are natural beings and so we must know that becoming effective doesn't happen without cooperation.

This oracle deck is designed to honor that reality. After you have learned your life purpose, do a quick spread to determine your powers.

Powers

The card you pull to represent your powers may seem obvious if you're already attuned to them, or it may be something you haven't yet developed. If this is the case, I highly recommend developing your gifts. Also, don't feel that you are limited by the card picked. You definitely have other powers, but the one chosen represents the most useful for you in this incarnation if you use and develop it.

Power of Each Realm

Nighttime Object Realm power can manifest as one or more of the following:

- The ability to "see" or sense spirits attached to plants, plant roots, certain dolls, statues, paintings, shrines, and other charmed objects in the dark or when the sun goes down using a special type of shamanic shadow vision (rare)
- The ability to make amulets and charms that are stronger than normal
- A special relationship to the dead

Physical Realm power can manifest as one or more of the following:

- An ability to take psychedelic mushrooms or other strong hallucinogens without fatigue or any dramatic side effects
- An ability to deeply tune into the intelligence of the body to speak to organs and tissues
- A solid body not negatively affected by hauntings and retrogrades
- A strong body that can perform athletically at a high level

Ethereal Realm power can manifest as one or more of the following:

- An ability to withstand the elements longer than most
- Having a strong vibration that activates the magic in others (folks known as "chargers")
- Giving life-changing hugs to people
- An ability to remember very fine details of a dream
- An ability to cook foods that energetically heal people
- An ability to smell entities or illness in the Ethereal Realm of others before they can manifest as illness in the physical body

Astral Realm power can manifest as one or more of the following:

- Heightened emotional awareness and wisdom
- Dramatically heightened emotional sensitivity
- The power to dream lucidly
- The ability to go on quests and do big healing for self and others in dream space
- The ability to jump out of the Astral Realm and astral project and astral travel
- The ability to bring amazing artwork from the astral plane

Mental Realm power can manifest as one or more of the following:

- The ability to stop pains or to heal parts of one's own body with only the mind
- The ability of extreme focus
- The ability to convince others of practically anything via thoughtform projection
- Great memory recall and mental organization
- A fast learner
- The ability to bless or curse through the eyes (via inner doll phenomena)

- Housing thought patterns that protect the integrity and power of spirit workers
- Strong "placebo effect" sensitivity
- Born to stretch the mind of rigid family beliefs

Intuitive Realm power can manifest as one or more of the following:

- The ability to use the light ray to psychically communicate with the light consciousness of plants during the day or night
- The ability to use the light ray to psychically communicate with the light consciousness of animals
- The ability to use the light ray to psychically communicate with the light consciousness of humans anywhere in the world
- The ability to channel the light ray through the heart space to feel the love of nature

Ancestral Realm power can manifest as one or more of the following:

- The natural ability to speak for your own blood ancestors through channeling
- The ability to recognize your authentic Indigenous culture

- The ability to pass down traditions exactly as they were done in the past
- The ability to channel the messages from gods praised in your bloodline

Coincidence Realm power can manifest as one or more of the following:

- Extreme luck manifesting through blessed synchronicity
- High divination abilities with tools such as shells, cards, or astrology
- A keen ability to find one's soul family

Mythic Realm power can manifest as one or more of the following:

- Prophetic insights that predict important events to come
- Miraculous healing using prayer, divine sounds, or hand symbols
- The ability to speak to beings from alternate star systems

HOW TO USE THIS DECK TO GET WHAT YOU WANT

If there is something you want, shuffle the deck and ask how you can get what you desire. When you choose a card, flip it over onto the table. To interpret the meaning, turn to the page of the book that corresponds to the card. Light a candle on your altar, and perform the ritual associated with that card for nine straight days while focusing on your desired outcome.

HOW TO USE THIS DECK TO FIGHT PROCRASTINATION

When procrastination hits us, it can be entirely frustrating. Many of us give into it and just start scrolling on our phones, staring at walls, or watching a show on our laptops. Deep down we know that we finally have time to work on that special project, but we just can't seem to put energy into it. There's always something that needs to be done around the house, or things we could be putting toward our jobs, or energy we could be pouring into all the people who want to show us their tasty distractions on social media. Why are we putting all those things above what we truly want? Why isn't there any energy to go for our deepest desire? The reason is starvation. There is a part of you that must be fed before you can get into it. This problem lies in one of the nine realms. Light some artemisia or palo santo, say a prayer, and shuffle this deck. Pull the top card to see which ritual can help and where the problem lies in general.

For example, if you pull "The Lovers," that card resonates with Realm 2, the Physical Realm. The issue is in something you must do physically. Gemini rules the card and also rules the lungs. So trying some deep breaths or guided meditation could be the answer to your problem. The Moon card also resonates with Realm 2, but the moon rules the waters. Your procrastination in this example could be based on your own dehydration.

THE ROYAL BLACK COURT

TO WHICH ROYAL FAMILY DO YOU BELONG?

We all belong to a royal family in the Astral Realm. It can be helpful to know which clan you belong to so that you can recognize them when they appear to you.

Take time to shuffle the deck and ask, "To which kingdom do I belong?" Place the deck down when you are led to stop shuffling, and pull cards until you see the first Royal Court card. This will be a king, queen, prince, or princess. The one you pull is your royal guide and an invitation to the elemental kingdom you truly belong to. The other cards that you picked before receiving a Royal Court card tell you the lessons and gifts that they will help you to work through in this life. The other cards show you the realms where you radiate the strongest. For example, let's say you shuffle the deck and pick The Moon card and The Star card before choosing the Princess of Earth. This means that the Princess of Earth has found you and recognized you as family and is walking you back to the land of Earth to meet the rest of the royals. These royals of Earth are going to be your guides in working through issues and developing your superpowers associated with The Star and The Moon cards. Once the link is made, these kings and queens can visit and work with you in your dreams as well as in other ways. Don't be surprised if they visit you in the dream space.

Royal Fire Clan	The Royal Fire Clan are the go-getters of the clans. They are also our fighters and heroes, the righteous who will always stand for what is right.
Royal Earth Clan	The Royal Earth Clan are the richest of them all. They store most of the money and financial luck in their zone. If you are in this clan, you definitely should ask where your abundance lies.
Royal Water Clan	The Royal Water Clan are the keepers of the deep mysteries. If you are looking for deep and mind-bending truths, this clan will suit you well.
Royal Air Clan	The Royal Air Clan houses the scribes and architects. Vast libraries of knowledge are stored there.

ANCESTRAL READING FOR
BLACK TRAUMA

WHAT TYPE OF ANCESTORS ARE
WALKING WITH YOU?

The Walking Tree Oracle is charged with the potential to link with all nine realms. This is powerful because many oracle decks are missing this ability to consciously direct the reader to the realm that will bring the most benefit— as if there is only one realm that surrounds us. No! We exist in a nine-realm superweb of endless potentialities. With most oracle decks, we shuffle and read the cards and just assume we are in contact with a monotonous spiritual plane of simplicity. No way! The realms are all very different! Some of them respect linear time, and others do not. This oracle will pull the Ancestral Realm right down to you. Start by lighting the candle on your oracle altar; this honors the Ethereal Realm but also lights the way for the ancestors to find you. Say your prayer and pick up your oracle deck. Look into the deck and pull out the Ancestors card. Set it up or lay it down near the candle. Get some water and drop small amounts into the cup while saying the names of your beloved ancestors. Place the card back in the deck, shuffle, and ask, "Which ancestors are standing with me today?"

Pull three cards and note if you pull a Major Arcana card or a Royal Court card.

If you pull a Royal Court card, that means that you have pulled a queen or king or prince or princess.

A Queen of Earth or Water means that there is an older female ancestor or past incarnation of self on your mother's side of the family walking with you.

A Queen of Fire or Air means that there is an older female ancestor or past incarnation of self on your father's side of the family walking with you.

A King of Earth or Water means that there is an older male ancestor or past incarnation of self on your mother's side of the family walking with you.

A King of Fire or Air means that there is an older male ancestor or past incarnation of self on your father's side of the family walking with you.

A Prince of Earth or Water means that there is a youthful male family member on your mother's side of the family walking with you. This could also mean a future relative or future self reaching back to walk with you.

A Prince of Fire or Air means that there is a youthful male ancestor on your father's side of the family walking with you. This could also mean a future relative or future self reaching back to walk with you.

A Princess of Earth or Water means that there is a youthful female ancestor on your mother's side of the family walking with you. This could also mean a future relative or self reaching back to walk with you.

A Princess of Fire or Air means that there is a youthful female ancestor on your father's side of the family walking with you. This could also mean a future relative or self reaching back to walk with you.

If out of those three cards, you pull at least one Major Arcana card, that card is the phase or issue/trauma they are here to help you with. Turn to the page of the book that corresponds to the Major Arcana card pulled and perform the ritual for nine consecutive days.

THE HIDDEN NATURE OF TREES AND THEIR BRANCHES

Trees are the strongest beings on earth. Some sages go as far as to say that what humans are to animals, trees are to plants. Trees conduct so much power that it's truly hard to comprehend. One tree branch with leaves attached is enough to send prayers blasting off through the messy cacophony of the city and deep into the multiverse. There are four types of tree spirits: healers, commanders, ghosts, and gurus.

Healers	Healers are often playful or serene spirits that bring a cool and calm vibration when experienced. They are called upon for lifting spirits and bringing a sense of peace and safety to a person. The eco-spiritual job of these trees is to push love into the air through their leaves after negative energies have been brought into the earth.

Commanders	Commander Trees are warrior types who are very serious and protective. They are called upon before a battle to instill courage and invincibility. The eco-spiritual job of these trees is to command, tighten, and stir up present stagnant energies that are close by.
Ghosts	Ghost Trees are the spirits of the haunted forest. They instill fear and grief for those who need to come to face with those things to evolve. These spirits have a sense of humor as well and like to play tricks that bring fear or madness. They are called upon for rites of passage and for the processing of fear and grief. The eco-spiritual job of these trees is to pull grief and fear into the earth so it can be transmuted. For this reason, many sad or grieving or troubled spirits are attracted to these trees.
Gurus	Guru Trees are the most diverse and mysterious. These trees are strict teachers that push the mind and spirit into areas of discomfort. The spirits always seem older and not impressed with childish ways of being. The eco-spiritual job of these trees is to push the energy of the forest as far out as it can go.

When you pull a card that sends you to one of these tree races, take a trip to a tree in your yard or a nearby park and see if there are any tree branches on the ground. If you can't find a grounded branch, ask the tree if it will be your helper for the issue at hand, and imagine or sense the answer. If there are no branches on the ground, just gather at least nine leaves from the tree and place them upon the home altar.

CARDS AND DESCRIPTIONS

The Walking Tree Oracle is a deck inspired by my experience with nine realms of existence, the traditional tarot, herbalism, African traditional religion, and astrology. The cards are:

Major Arcana			
Card	*Planet*	*Zodiac*	*Realm*
0 The Fool	Uranus	Aquarius	8
1 The Magician	Mercury	Gemini	4
2 The High Priestess	Moon	Pisces	9
3 The Empress	Venus	Taurus	3
4 The Emperor	Mars	Scorpio	6
5 The Hierophant	Venus	Taurus	1
6 The Lovers	Mercury	Gemini	2
7 The Chariot	Moon	Cancer	4
8 Wooden Heart	Sun	Leo	6
9 The Hermit	Mercury	Virgo	7
10 The Wheel	Jupiter	Sagittarius	8
11 Justice	Venus	Libra	6

Major Arcana				
	Card	Planet	Zodiac	Realm
12	The Hanged Man	Neptune	Pisces	5
13	Death	Mars	Scorpio	7
14	Temperance	Jupiter	Sagittarius	5
15	The Trickster	Saturn	Capricorn	2
16	The Tower	Mars	Aries	5
17	The Star	Uranus	Aquarius	3
18	The Moon	Moon	Cancer	2
19	The Sun	Sun	Leo	3
20	Judgment	Mars	Aries	9
21	The World	Saturn	Capricorn	8
22	Osain	Moon	Cancer	1
23	Jiridon	Moon	Cancer	4
24	Bear Tree	Earth	all signs	9
25	Ancestors	Pluto	Scorpio	7
26	Mother of God	Venus	Taurus	9
27	Ghost Tree	Pluto	Scorpio	1
28	Healing Tree	Venus	Libra	6
29	Commander Tree	Mars	Aries	5
30	Guru Tree	Saturn	Aquarius	9
31	The Stranger	Venus	Taurus	5
32	The Unicorn	Neptune	Pisces	9
33	Sankofa	Saturn	Aquarius	7

Royal Court	
I	King of Earth
II	Queen of Earth
III	Prince of Earth
IV	Princess of Earth
V	King of Air
VI	Queen of Air
VII	Prince of Air
VIII	Princess of Air
IX	King of Fire
X	Queen of Fire
XI	Prince of Fire
XII	Princess of Fire
XIII	King of Water
XIV	Queen of Water
XV	Prince of Water
XVI	Princess of Water

MAJOR ARCANA

0. THE FOOL—NOTHING

Realm:	Planet:	Zodiac:	Herb:
8	Uranus	Aquarius	basil

This card is telling you that any path will do. Take a step in any direction based on the paths provided, and activate your story. There may be some fear at starting this new path or even some naysayers in your ears, but The Fool will win if he can simply ignore them. The fool ignores the masses and follows the beat of his own drum. The fool wins through play. By moving in his unique way, he activates the harmonies and synchronicities in the Realm of Coincidence. As the seemingly careless and naive fool moves toward the edge of the cliffs, he is protected.

Card Meanings

Being fully open, embracing the now. New energy. Taking a chance even though things aren't all the way figured out. Moving to the route less traveled. Taking chances and risks. The beginning of the journey after a move of the heart. Next step in a direction after fully completing a mission or initiation. The one who seems foolish will be okay.

If this card is your Mission on Earth, stay loose, playful, and open and don't let the naysayers kill your vibe.

Reverse

Do not appear foolish or behave as though you can move without planning. Your heart is not in the right place to make choices based on the heart. Your infatuation could lead you to your doom.

Practice 1

Go into your bathroom, light a candle, and think about your life while taking nine deep breaths. Hop into the shower and dance and/or sing wildly as the water hits you. Sing whatever nonsense comes to mind, and take note of what messages come out. If the message is pure nonsense, that's good, too! When it is raining outside, do the same while dancing in the street or playfully jumping or stomping in any puddles.

Practice 2

Paint, draw, or write the absolute ugliest or worst piece of work you've ever produced. Carelessly do the work. Look at what you've produced and laugh at it.

Herbal Work

Take some basil and wear it around your neck. Also be mindful if you randomly run into the plant or a dish or tea or salad prepared with basil. See the basil during this time as a charm for good luck but also confirmation that you are on the right track.

Tea: basil

1. THE MAGICIAN—KNOWLEDGE

Realm:	Planet:	Zodiac:	Herb:
4	Mercury	Gemini	mugwort

A handsome Black man appears in your sight, and you see all the phases of the moon in his face. He is completely refreshed, perhaps eternally. He is the owner of all the moon phases. Like Tehuti (Thoth), the Kemetic god of wisdom, he is a spirit of Mercury but also of the moon. He is a true magician, able to use all of the moon phases to his benefit. He is a time master. He is ever aware and present in the shadows. This card works strongly with dream space: All roads converge in the astral dream realm of fruit and honey. This realm is the spice of life, the fruit that is eaten from all realms by beings during what we know as sleep. Every dimension converges here for water and refreshment despite their level of awareness.

Card Meanings

The ability to birth your dreams from the astral plane into the realm of matter is on the horizon. Many of the tools you need—tools of fire, earth, air, and water—are being revealed in your dreams to let you know that they are already within your reach. Record and analyze the messages from your dreams in order to give clues to your Conscious Mind. The tools are there; all you must do is own them and begin to practice. This card also corresponds to the pineal gland, which acts as a Mercurial messenger linking the brain to the cosmos. Nightly travel into the realm of dreams is essential for a sound mind. This card represents the part of you that goes to dream space and becomes a container to bring astral/dream nourishment and messages back to the body while you are sleeping. The magician is alert and incredibly intellectual only because of his healthy balance with the other side.

As a Mission on Earth, this card tells you to stay active, alert, wise, and always collecting new tools. With that being said, do not let your energy become too scattered. Focus and dedication lead to success.

Reverse

General imbalance between sleeping and waking. You do not have the tools or the right things in position to act. Your mind is not in the right place.

Practice 1

Drink rosemary tea and then pray for assistance. Sleep with a cup of water and a notebook next to you. Write your dreams as soon as you awaken. Make sure you are honoring the dreams by saying a gratitude prayer when you awaken. If you feel clear about the meaning, change something in your waking life based on the dream you had. You can also choose to do something symbolically to honor your dream such as feed a cat because you dreamed of a starving cat, for example.

Practice 2

Ignite your creative juices through creating a vision board that brings your hopes and dreams to light.

Herbal Work

Say a prayer and drink a good dream herb before bed for
nine consecutive nights. Any plants or animals seen in
these dreams should be noted as current allies. Place symbols or plants or dried herbs representing these allies upon
your main in-home altar.

Tea: rosemary leaf

2. THE HIGH PRIESTESS—WISDOM

Realm:	Planet:	Zodiac:	Herb:
9	Moon	Pisces	motherwort

A woman in trance experiences herself in a state of total
peace. She becomes a small tree, and leaves sprout from
where her ears would be. She's amazed that for the first
time she can hear light. She experiences her body as being
everything on earth, and her face can only witness all the
incredible miracles that have been imprinted in the etheric
imprint of the earth. Reiki symbols, mass sightings of the
Virgin de Guadalupe, and all miraculous healings appear
in front of her face. She sees the impossible, the Savior, the
great harmonizer, the lost healing technologies of earth.

Card Meanings

Call upon the blessings of the most holy spirit, the most
holy and high that you know. A miracle is close by. Have

faith that the sign or the teacher is coming. There is not a whole bunch of work that you need to do. Even if you do find a teacher, there is not hard work involved. This is more about receptivity and moving in a tranquil flowstate. Become attuned and vibrate at the same frequency as your teachers.

There's no need to fight anything. Healing is the only thing needed.

If your Mission on Earth card is the High Priestess, move in faith, grace, and holiness. Keep your body pure of too many substances such as MSG and other toxins that can block your channel. This is a very light energy that should not be blocked or bogged down. Be careful and intentional of what you place upon your mind and spirit.

Reverse

Your intuition is leading you astray. Move in practicality and sure knowledge instead of resonance. Follow a pattern, that which has been tested. Follow rules. You can't just feel your way through this situation.

Practice

When the night falls, go on a walk while fully focused on the moon. Let your intuition lead your steps. If the moon is present, say a prayer through the moon and into the deepest reaches of space. If the moon is full, etch your own symbol onto the moon's surface. Do this in your mind's eye. With no moon present, simply hold gratitude in your heart as you meditate in the spot in the park or forest that you reached.

Herbal Work

For nine consecutive nights with 9 tablespoons of salt, make a strong motherwort tea and pour it in a bucket of cold water. Take a shower while praying and then turn the shower off. Dump the pail of cold water over your head and air dry.

Tea: 1 part lemon balm, 3 parts skullcap, 3 parts oatstraw

3. THE EMPRESS—UNDERSTANDING

Realm:	Planet:	Zodiac:	Herb:
3	Venus	Taurus	damiana

The Empress is a great tree mother and goddess rooted in love and loyalty and earth. She sits tall with life in her belly, carrying the keys to nourishment, legitimization, and manifestation. She is the cycle, the law, and the reality of what must be done for optimal physical health. This also puts her into position as a type of doctor or nutritionist who seeks to keep everyone's foundations in alignment. She wants to know if you ate mineral-dense meals and chose the very best fruits and vegetables you can get your hands on. She is the mother who also is sure to put tons of love into her food when she cooks it. She is one who knows that beauty is also medicine. When the food is prepared, it should also be beautiful to look at. She is always making sure that she is as beautiful as she can be through eating in a balanced way, adding flowers to her hair, dancing in fine garments, and showing up fully in every moment. She is a magnetic and grounding force that normalizes and sustains.

As the wife of the Emperor, she offers protection and a place to manifest creation so that he can play the role of enforcer. He needs the Empress. It's her steadiness, patience, selfless dedication, and consistency that make his work take shape. The Empress embodies the materials for all that will manifest. She is Mother Earth and the sustainer of all the earth's angelic forces. To understand the Empress is to understand manifestation and care.

Card Meanings

This is the time for generosity, processing those creative juices, and giving birth! Share your abundance! Push those projects and manifest what is yours into this world so it can give to you the beauty of the world. Your work and your life both need nutrients and energy. Give yourself over to eating healthy, life-rich foods cooked with love. Qigong, yoga, taiji, and religious dancing all increase life force. The mind needs support from the body and can't find peace until you honor your body, which needs nourishment. Give your body over to the healing herbal plant constituents.

If you are one of the people who has pulled this card as a Mission on Earth, you'll need to carry yourself as an Empress should. High integrity and abundance are the name of the game. Once you tap into your abundance, generosity with sustainability is the next goal.

Reverse

Scarcity, disconnection from the body, poverty.

Practice

The Empress is an energy that cares about the energy levels of the body. Do you know what your body really wants? Sit under a tree, preferably a linden, or a tree that intuitively pulls you in. Imagine that your entire body is a tongue with a mouth all around. As a tongue, your entire body can feel taste. Picture a sour bubble exploding right above your head. Allow the flavor of sour to rain upon you, and take in its flavor all over the body. If it makes you tremble, you should tremble. Whatever movement or sound comes out of you, allow it. Once the sensation passes, move through the same process with bitter, salty, and sweet. After you've gone through the flavors, ask the tree that you are sitting under to balance your vibrations so that you may be fully in tune with what your body really needs. When you feel a warmth in your heart space, this meditation is finished. Keep in mind that this card signifies a time to eat life-giving foods such as fruit and fresh veggies.

Herbal Work

Drink damiana tea for nine consecutive days in the evening. You can also strain damiana into your bath water and allow seven to nine roses to float in the water with you. It can really add to this work if you dress all the way up as if you are trying to seduce someone with your attractiveness. You are amazing. For nine days, seduce yourself.

Tea: 3 parts red raspberry, 3 parts holy basil, 3 parts nettles

4. THE EMPEROR— CULTURE AND HEALING TOOLS

Realm:	Planet:	Zodiac:	Herb:
6	Mars	Scorpio	osha

The Emperor is a force to behold! He is assertive, strong, and commanding. His movements are relaxed yet bold as a result of deep knowledge, wisdom, and understanding. The Elk doesn't move timidly. The Elk bursts into the meadow, branches from trees flying to earth as he proudly moves to the stream. The Emperor is like the Elk. He can move boldly because his moves are appropriate and generate more life, especially the actions that appear to be destructive.

The Emperor is like the great King Solomon, who reached deep into the world of the great mysteries. The Emperor has found power there. He is not shaken up by any ghosts, goblins, or things that go bump in the night. He's not afraid of naysayers and those who wish to see him fail. He has found power in knowing where his help and power truly lie.

His plant guardians—the hawthorn, aspen, osha, and juniper—have roots and branches with living leaves tied to his spirit. His living shrines cloak him in power. His crystals stabilize him, and his relationships make up for his weaknesses while charging his strengths. He is solid and ready to push forward, always manifesting as a fierce king!

The Emperor is in position to move mountains. He has an Empress who recognized him as her husband and promoted him. She is the throne, the badge, the temple, and the ultimate legitimizer. The Emperor can accomplish anything and experience boundless energy while resting upon the foundation of love, nourishment, stability, and rank that manifests inside and outside of him as the Empress. Her love gives him focus, her power keeps him covered, and her presence keeps him accountable. The Emperor is extremely strong because the Empress is always by his side keeping distractions, perversion, illness, and defilement at bay.

Card Meanings

The guides are with you. You can see it in the markings. Fight as if you have a million warriors with you. The bear spirits are here feeding you with the strength to push down trees and step through piercing branches. Clear your path. Fight and push the threat away. You have access to the position and protection you need!

As a Mission on Earth, this card poses challenges. This is what being the Emperor is all about: learning how to face those challenges by standing in authenticity. The young Emperor may want to hide behind titles and policies until he has grown. When he is mature, he stands upon his inner authority and what he knows to be right.

Reverse

You are not in a place to defend yourself. Play it safe. Play the game safely and quietly. You need accountability. Recklessness.

Practice

Go to a nearby park. Kneel down in a group of trees and make a solid oath to them. Feel the power radiating from your heart and to your knee and then deep into the earth. Feel that power radiating far outward to all the surrounding trees. Connect with them. Tell them your sworn oath to be a medicinal force in the world. You may feel a slight shift in your spirit. Once you do, rise from that spot into a standing position. Go to the tree you feel most drawn to and grab a small branch with the leaves still attached. Take it home with you and place it above your bed. Keep a few leaves in your pockets for protection as well.

Herbal Work

If you pull this card, you want to work with the aspen tree, the hawthorn tree, juniper tree, palm tree, mango tree, banana tree, or any other tree branches that are both benevolent and protective. Sleep near to these types of trees for messages, or bring a branch into the home and sleep near to it. Wear protective roots in your daily life and while sleeping. Carry a quartz crystal that was buried near an oak tree into your next intense emotional battle.

Tea: hibiscus

5. THE HIEROPHANT—POWER

Realm:	Planet:	Zodiac:	Herb:
1	Venus	Taurus	kola nut

The Hierophant has a wife. This wife is "the people," and he must remain dedicated and loyal to her. His powers lie in his ability to remain grounded, consistent, traditional, and objective. His ways are earthy and regular like the Babalawo. He is not an open channel for spirits. He is concerned with reading the divination correctly, maintaining order in ceremony, and making sure the deities are properly kept through the work with shrines.

Card Meanings

You are being called to follow the tradition of your ancestors and to become grounded. The power that comes with being grounded will bring you freedom. You may also want to consult a trusted Babalawo or priest of your faith to have a general check-in or even to ask some pressing questions. This card may be telling you to talk with your high parental network so you can mentor more effectively. You may need to declutter your altar or to work more closely with a particular shrine. This is a card of parental love and proper boundaries. When a priest or teacher takes on a student or disciple, they become a parental figure over that person. It is strongly prohibited that priests act on romantic feelings for their students. Being ruled by Venus, the Hierophant represents heaven on earth. This is very attractive to others seeking salvation, and they will want to fall in love with him. It is the responsibility of the Hierophant to be unfazed and to bring that love to a higher level. If he is not able to do that, he must never meet with that student in private or he must cut that student off. This card teaches the beauty in sacrifice.

If this card is pulled as your Mission on Earth, you'll find that you are constantly in stories that revolve around the proper use of trust, power, and mentorship.

Reverse

Abuse of power, improper boundaries between student and teacher, dogmatic thinking working against client, closed-minded.

Practice

Go outside in a natural space and lie on your back. Absorb earth energy into your body, and feel yourself becoming more grounded. If you are near one or more trees, pay close attention to the tree(s) from that view. Notice how much more you can see when grounded, seeing a more complete picture. When the spirit leads you, close your eyes, keeping the trees in mind. Place your hands over your chest and chant, "I will never betray my heart." Lie a few moments longer, then go back home.

Herbal Work

Grab nine leaves from an oak tree or pine or kapok, and stack three silver dollars on top of the leaves. Light a cigar or all-natural tobacco cigarette, and blow smoke on the leaves and coins nine times while visualizing the unlocking of stagnant ancestral wealth. Say your prayer and walk away.

Tea: star anise

6. THE LOVERS—EQUALITY

Realm:	Planet:	Zodiac:	Herb:
2	Mercury	Gemini	linden

Two trees kiss each other lovingly in the forest. The two trees become lovers through the rustling of the wind. The tree branches are the vocal cords of the tree people. When the trees wish to sing, applaud, or talk, the leaves begin to shimmer. A divine gust of wind will just come out of nowhere and carry whatever they wish to express.

Card Meanings

This is a card about communication and twin flames. Your twin flame manifested as a person, pet, job, event, or some other opportunity is nearby. This card could be telling you to work with someone or compromise as well. This card is also a sexual card, as it relates to the realm of bodies. This card could also ask partners to become much more passionate in their lovemaking: more breathing and expressing. This card could also imply looking into Daoist or yogic sexual practices to deepen sexual intimacy.

This card is also saying that sometimes the best way to know what you really think is to run your thoughts by another person who loves you. The wisdom will start to spill out of you.

If this is your Mission on Earth, you must find love. In that real love, you must find the trust to allow that person(s) to love you out of yourself into new, beautiful realities and deeper truths. It is important in this lifetime not to project yourself onto others, but to truly love and see people as they are.

Reverse

Too reliant on a partner. Go alone.

Practice

Take a loving walk with your romantic partner. When you feel led to stop, ask your partner to gaze lovingly at you to charge your connection. Tell them what's in your heart. If you are single, you can do the same exercise in a platonic way with a friend. Tell that friend how much you appreciate them. If you have no friend nearby, take a seat under a linden tree or a tree you feel drawn to, and take deep breaths. Use your imagination to visualize this whole exercise in your heart. Tell your spiritual double how you feel about them. Do not be afraid to speak to your spiritual double out loud.

Herbal Work

Use mullein leaf tea to honor the proper flow of oxygen through the lungs. Place mullein leaves in the soles of your shoes for nine consecutive days.

Tea: linden with honey

7. THE CHARIOT—GOD WITHIN

Realm:	Planet:	Zodiac:	Herb:
4	Moon	Cancer	kava

A tree emerges from between two sides of a woman. One is dark like nighttime with stars in her skin. The other is light with rays like daytime solar magic. When the conscious mind and the subconscious mind work together in harmony, there is a greater capacity for joy. Creativity and production are guaranteed when polarities work together. Where there is an edge, many things are possible.

Card Meanings

At times, your capacities seem terribly limited, but you are not one-dimensional. You are truly not an "I." You are a "we." Be careful about which voice you identify as an "I," because it can keep you from realizing your other truths. Expand your perception of self, and go into the deepest recesses of your emotions. You do not need to let the demons within the subconscious keep you bound. Rise above emotion into the thinking of your inner god self. This card asks you to hold strong to righteousness no matter how much the emotions tug on you. Procrastination is not your friend. Scattered energy and suppression are also not your friends. Reach within and fight your way to the top! It is important to be able to accept the sides of yourself that you may see as nondesirable without harsh judgment. There are gifts in that clear, nonemotional awareness, such as being able to identify which side of yourself is speaking at any given moment. It's also good to know what areas you may need assistance with. This is impossible to know if you've never looked at your weaknesses to understand them. Hypnosis can also be helpful here. Not being defensive about what others reveal about you while in your dark spaces is incredibly useful. Choose not to be defensive of sides of yourself you can't see. Trust those you love. It can also be good to choose a "muck partner," a friend or someone you can scream and yell and process in front of in a raw and emotional way.

If the Chariot is your Mission on Earth, expect a lifetime that is going to help you to learn how to work with all kinds of emotions in ways that are medicinal to yourself and those around you.

Reverse

Let your muses lead you. Take a break. Give in to your emotional wants. Your emotions should be the leader. Sit in the shadow and observe. Do not fight against the current!

Practice 1

Time is not a linear trajectory with disappearing moments fading into the distant past. Everything that has happened is part of you and has made an imprint upon time-space and on your emotional body. Take time to go within and ask the younger versions of yourself if they are okay. Perhaps your seven-year-old self may ask for something. If that is the case, use your imagination and your inner eye to go within and be with that inner child. See what it needs or asks for, even if it is just a blessing or a hug.

Go into this deep space to remove negative soul plants that project badly on the way you see your world.

Practice 2

Meet with your muck partner (preferably in the middle of nowhere) for one night or three consecutive nights (for a serious issue) and say how you really feel about a situation that is bothering you. Scream, yell, punch the air, curse, throw a tantrum, throw objects, and say mean or insensitive things you don't really mean while your partner times you for three 9-minute periods. In between those periods, let your partner spend 3 minutes explaining what they heard. After all three rounds, clearly plan the next steps for 15 minutes and walk away feeling purged.

Herbal Work

Drink kava root tea and either paint or draw one aspect of yourself. Pray over the one that you end up drawing. Kava is an amazing tea to help soothe the ache of painful emotions. Be with this tea when grief or emotions are too much.

Tea: kava root, cloves, cinnamon sticks with almond milk

8. WOODEN HEART—
STRENGTH TO BUILD

Realm:	Planet:	Zodiac:	Herb:
6	Sun	Leo	hawthorn

The pain and the longing for what was lost can leave us paralyzed or depressed until the heart realizes that it is stronger. The energy of the trees' strong wood is now in the blood. This medicine was accumulated from every tree and every plant medicine you've ever touched. It moves to the heart to provide hardness and structure for understanding and power.

Card Meanings

You are becoming solid. You can handle the tests that are coming your way. You don't need to try to control anything through force. Just show up and do what feels genuine. Your heart knows what to do.

If this card is your Mission on Earth, you'll be shown time and time again that there are times when the mind will be pushed to the max and the heart will simply take over and shine light in areas you once saw as hopeless. This path teaches trust in self and lessons of the heart.

Reverse

You may not be ready for the test ahead.

Practice

Take a walk to a nearby tree and press your palms into the bark of the tree. Take nine deep breaths. Picture a golden light coming from the tree and going to your heart. Allow the light to strengthen your heart. Allow the heart to also develop a light wooden covering that blocks out all prickly negativity from harming its softness. Feel the heart shining, strengthened and restored. Take nine deep breaths and release.

Herbal Work

The hawthorn tree is an amazing ally for the strengthening of the spiritual heart. If a hawthorn tree is near you, try sleeping or lying in meditation under this tree while focusing on the spiritual heart, the emotional heart, and the physical heart. If a hawthorn tree is not near you, you can summon some of its power by going to any tree of choice and pouring water upon the tree while summoning the spirit of the hawthorn. Say, "Hawthorn (pour water), Hawthorn (pour water), Hawthorn be with me (pour water)." I recommend doing this while working with the hawthorn tree as well to stir it up and put it in an active state for spiritual work. While lying there under the tree, dedicate at least nine deep breaths or 5 minutes to each of the three hearts.

While in the presence of the sun, drink some oatstraw, picturing the sun rays going straight to your heart chakra.

Tea: oatstraw, red raspberry, and holy basil

9. THE HERMIT—DESTROY

Realm:	Planet:	Zodiac:	Herb:
7	Mercury	Virgo	white willow

The Hermit says his final words before he retreats into his magical world of study. Who knows when the people will see him again. The one thing that is for sure is that he will reappear at the right time. After performing miracles and keeping the people connected to their spirits for a time, he must go within himself to study and work upon his inner worlds.

This is his time to retreat into his library and plan his next steps. His ancestors will meet with him privately from within his own soul as he moves through the activation that will take place from reading the sacred texts of masters. He will read old journals written by his ancestors and himself from years past. The Hermit is a carrier of the ancient ways. He is an eternal student.

Card Meanings

Your ancestors are speaking from within you. Words, books, and study will activate their desires within you. This is the time to retreat from the world and work on your projects in secret. Planning, dedication, and critical thinking will lead you closer to your desired goal.

A Hermit Mission on Earth is an often-lonely life path. Much study, time in solitude, and introspection are necessary to put forth the medicine deep within you.

Reverse

Keep nothing secret and make sure there are eyes on your projects.

Practice

Say a quick prayer and then open to a random page of one of your favorite wisdom books. If you wish to take things a step further, choose three or seven books, lay them in a circle around you, and spin nine times. With your eyes closed, kneel down and pick up the book in front of you. Open your eyes and read the title. This is the book you want. Read the chapter that calls to you or at least nine pages of it and see what stirs inside of you. Meditate or write in your journal.

Herbal Work

Burn some palo santo, place some rosemary oil on your third eye, and meditate while listening to your ancestral language. If you do not know it, channel it from the ancestral realms. If you don't know how to do this, just imagine what it may sound like and randomly speak gibberish in ways that touch your heart. Document how this makes you feel when you've completed the meditation.

Tea: elder berry

10. THE WHEEL—COSMIC AND RADIANT

Realm:	Planet:	Zodiac:	Herb:
8	Jupiter	Sagittarius	holy basil

Everything good is swirling around you to birth the most abundant reality so that you can experience a juicy era that is full of life. Whatever is good for you is swirling around you, waiting for you to interact. Your body of synchronicity is healthy, and all your movements in life are flowing and moving gracefully.

Card Meanings

Good luck is aggressively seeking you. Achieve inner stillness to know what is in front of you so you don't miss it!

This is a very lucky Mission on Earth card. Spend this life creating "machines" and "vessels" in order to capture all the luck constantly wanting to shower you. If you don't have machines to process the blessings, they will remain as unusable raw material. If you don't have vessels to catch the blessings, they'll just absorb back into the earth. Once you make the right machine or vessel, you can't lose. This life path is about finding the key machines and vessels to carry many blessings.

Reverse

Bad luck. Curses. Beware of accidents.

Practice

In this practice, you will be looking for a signal. Meditate among trees for a few minutes with The Wheel card in mind. Stand up and walk until you cross paths with a stranger. If there are no strangers, let your signal be the sight of a bird either in your mind or in external reality. Take note of the stranger (if you find one) or the bird, and find a spot to sit. Visualize the stranger or the bird shape-shifting into a wheel in your own heart. Feel the wheel slowly begin to spin. Let this wheel spin faster and faster until you can feel yourself becoming a magnet for all the blessings you've refused to allow yourself to receive. Feel all the goodness coming to you like winds blowing waters from heaven upon you. Lastly, take a deep breath and picture those waters falling into containers. Open your eyes and write down what those containers look like. Write down the containers in your life that could be tightened up so you can receive the blessings that you have called your way.

Herbal Work

Eat basil or drink basil as tea while making a wish. Pour out some tea by the door of a place that represents where you'd like to see a change. If the matter is financial, do it at a bank; if it is a health problem, do it at a hospital; and so on.

Tea: holy basil

11. JUSTICE—THE SCALES

Realm:	Planet:	Zodiac:	Herb:
6	Venus	Libra	yarrow

Maat is the balance-keeper in the cosmos. She is also the great thermometer of God. The scales that she brings are the final and highest tool of decision making in the multiverse. Maat is also the idea that there is a divine path for each and every one of us. At our death, our hearts will be placed on a scale and measured against the feather of Maat. If the heart is heavier than the feather, that means that we allowed the world to bog down our purpose.

Card Meanings

You pulled this card because your actions matter. There is no positive change coming unless you examine your heart and follow a straight and narrow compass. If you can follow the feather of truth, you can find amazing power and luck. The universe will support you if you can move in clarity and within the powers of your highest purpose. You may find that you are in a state of being tested. Push forward in faith and in truth. This is not the time to pursue only what you crave. This is the time to move with a sober and learned mind. The foolhardy will not be supported even if they move with the best intentions. If you want something, be in the right places with the right mindset.

If this is your Mission on Earth path, you will need to use discernment to bring balance to your inner landscape as well as your environment. You will need to be the person to step back and step out of ego to do and say what is best for a situation. This will take practice, so don't be too hard on yourself in the beginning. The best starting point is to take a breath, check in with yourself, and see options where others see only dead ends. This will be a major theme in your life.

Reverse

Imbalanced morals. Chaotic ways.

Practice

Light a candle and sit in silence. Move your attention to the center of the heart. Enter into the halls of your heart. You may see a power animal or a guide. Follow that guide to the hall of Maat (the hall of the deity represented on the Justice card). Move into the beautiful temple alone and see the scales in front of you. One side of the scales holds a feather. Your own heart appears on the other side. Are the scales balanced? If not, ask Maat what needs to be done to find balance. Maat may speak; she also may just give you a look. Either way, open your eyes, pick up your phone, and call three people in your life of any age, asking if they need help with anything. Schedule a time to meet with at least one of them, and hold to your commitment.

Herbal Work

Drink or burn some yarrow while lighting a seven-day candle. Pay attention to how the candle burns. If there is a black film on the glass, repeat the work until it burns clean. You are clearing away bad luck.

Tea: yarrow

12. THE HANGED MAN—ESCAPE

Realm:	Planet:	Zodiac:	Herb:
5	Neptune	Pisces	skullcap

The peaceful rest of a floating island. Your eyes are focused inward; your nose is the source of the flowing wind. Take a breath through your nose and feel the winds crash down upon the tops of your lips. Your lips are the restful lands. You aren't upon the floating island. You *are* the floating island.

Card Meanings

You are being asked to emotionally disconnect from the situation. It will take some time and distance to re-prioritize where your energy should go. It is okay to disappear in order to find your peace and stillness. People don't need to always know where you are. You don't have to answer your phone; place your energy elsewhere. It is also important to note here that your loudest thought isn't always the one that will bring you peace. Sit back and take a broader look at this situation. You don't have to react or give in to ego. You don't even need what you perceive to be "the facts." This is bigger than what your current waking dream knows to be true. Put your notions of fact and truth aside, and focus on developing the realities that have proved to bring the most peace within. You have more mental choices than you know. Acknowledge your emotions but refuse to act upon them. Go on a silent vacation into your own mind. Build something there alone, and escape from the battles and rat races around you.

As a Mission on Earth card, the Hanged Man speaks about a life of retreat. Even if you enjoy hard work, that is not the reason that you incarnated. You incarnated to take it easy and show others how to do the same when they need to. You will need to know when to retreat to be healthy in this life. You may find that you have a hard time fully locking into any path fully. The gift in this is that you have full freedom to choose where you spiritually want to be. This life path warns against finding ways to escape that are harmful or deadly.

Reverse

If you do nothing, you will fail.

Practice 1

Deep breaths, especially through the nostrils, are indicated here. Take nine deep breaths through the nostrils, and breathe out through the mouth. When you breathe in, hold for at least 3 seconds before releasing for at least 3 seconds. Make sure you are relaxed and allowing your belly to fill with air. See yourself as a floating island. You can see your human self in the world below. Your human self needs your assistance. Allow yourself to drop a rope to the lowlands and lift your human self up to the heavens to experience peace upon you, the floating island. Tell your human self they can come to you, the floating island, anytime for a peaceful break.

Practice 2

Take a walk and make it a point to take in the smells. Smell any flowers or tree barks or even the aromas of restaurants as you walk by. Breathe deeply and take each smell deep into the heart. If it is too cold to go outside, smell several essential oils or spices from the spice cabinet for a reset. Sit with each smell for nine consecutive deep breaths before moving to the next.

Herbal Work

Take some skullcap tincture throughout the day. You need to repair damaged nerve cells. This herb will also help you to let go of constrictive thoughtforms.

Tea: skullcap

13. DEATH—END OF CYCLE

Realm:	Planet:	Zodiac:	Herb:
7	Mars	Scorpio	onion

The Phoenix woman has let go of her latest form. She has shed her old skin and released everything. The cycle for her new life has begun. The old body is no longer necessary. She faced her fears and didn't even try to hold on. She knew it was coming. She had to be honest about what truly belonged to her and let go of anything else. She loved the body, but seasons change. The only thing that she could take with her to the next mission was the fire within. The body died. The blessings of the body decayed. The curses of the body are no more. She has transitioned.

Card Meanings

The time has come to die. Another version of yourself is ready to be born. The winter has come, and the cycle is complete. It is time for something to go. It may be something inside of you or a situation outside of you. The time is missed for now, the season is over, and the letting go must begin. Say your "goodbyes" and get ready for the deepest sleep. The dream must take new shape. Some things must be shelved until the season swings back around. For now, prepare for the next phase. You have no choice. The universe has chosen to move on. This card warns that one should stand in the integrity of the ending phase of a season. This is done by refusing to hold on when it is time for the season to pass. If your integrity can't accept the facts and take part in the ending of the season, your inner demons, the malefic parts of you, will spill out and do it for you. In other words, throw out the old milk before it starts to smell bad. The phase will end one way or another.

If this card manifests as a result of a Mission on Earth Spread, it's speaking about the importance of transitions and the endings of cycles. There can be much peace in this life path when a person learns that relationships are like plants. Some are like the bristlecone pine, everlasting, while other plants are beautiful annuals and biennials, meant to live only a short time. Many beautiful relationships operate in the same way. They are only meant to be short and sweet. So letting go in gratitude is important. Building a greater capacity to hold large amounts of gratitude for all the beauty that comes and goes in a life leads to great joy. Proper death is only a change, the proper ending of a cycle.

Reverse

Hold on to who you are and what you have at all costs!

Practice

Stop what you are doing and go to sleep. When you awaken, get rid of things that have served their purpose.

Trust your intuition and be completely honest. Old shoes you never wear, give them away. Creepy paintings or dolls or statues that give you bad vibes, let them go.

Herbal Work

Drink a strong decoction of onion three times a day. Wear garlic around the neck for a day to ward off death, illness, and energetic vampires. For added protection, sleep under a branch of elder leaves for three consecutive nights to ward off evils.

Tea: onion, elder flowers

14. TEMPERANCE—BALANCE

Realm:	Planet:	Zodiac:	Herb:
5	Jupiter	Sagittarius	mint

The wise one knows that balance is key. Choose the middle path!

Card Meanings

This card tells us that we can't always lean on what we have inside. Sometimes we need assistance or accountability from friends, family, experts, or nature's healers (herbs) and that is okay. We all need somebody to lean on. The right people can offer a community that can hold you accountable. Let the thoughts of those you trust influence you now. What is both firmly rooted and good that can keep your mind from falling? Do you need herbs or minerals? Do you need to wear a certain stone? Do you need another opinion? Find the support you need to maintain your mental balance! This card warns also against being bullied by the randomness of a day or by the weight of a project. There shouldn't even be one day when a project keeps you from going outside to greet the sun and smell the roses. There should never be a day when a project you are working on forces you to push away a great opportunity so you can merely procrastinate and be drained by the project's harsh vibration. This card says that you should also never let endless small tasks keep you from adding some piece to that big goal you wish to complete. This card is about listing and honoring those golden time blocks. Blocks are important. You can't build a castle without them.

This Mission on Earth is a balancing act. It is a life path that is going to shape you to look at balancing in ways that honor the long term. This also includes the finishing of those years-long passion projects. But projects like these can't come to fruition without pattern recognition, vision, and balancing the many dimensions of self.

Reverse
Delusion, not the result of anything truly magical.

Practice

Making space: This card is calling you to create regular and recurring time blocks for your gifts. There's not a greater gift you can give to yourself right now. Immediately sit down with a pen and a calendar and block out time for a project near and dear to your heart. You can choose your block to be 30 minutes before you'd regularly wake up or 10 minutes after you get off work. You should stick to whatever block is created and find the discipline to turn off your phone and block out as many distractions as you can until the block's time has ended. Hold this block pattern for as many days as you need to accomplish a goal.

Herbal Work

It's time to get in tune with mint. Peppermint, spearmint … doesn't matter. Drink mint daily. Host a party and be sure to serve mint tea to every guest.

Tea: mint

15. THE TRICKSTER—CAPTURE

Realm:	Planet:	Zodiac:	Herb:
2	Saturn	Capricorn	alfalfa

Anansi the spider god is a trickster and a truth teller. He came to us when his people were brought to the Americas. He carries all the tools that the African has had to use to survive in a game rigged against him. The game of survival is a rough place.

Anansi is a survivor that knows how to hustle and fool others to make up for what he lacks.

Card Meanings

Anansi tells us that we can win despite the chains. He explains that these chains were always breakable. He spins a web leading us into the chemistry of our own minds so that we have roads to find keys. The breaking of the chains starts in the mind. Addictions, relationships, contracts, morals, values, and goals should all be examined from time to time. We do this to make sure that we aren't lost in the maze of life or just going in circles. We should be spiraling and not circling. Build your web, and stick to your plan at all costs. This is a card of survival by any means. Addictions to people, places, and substances can also pop up with this card.

As a Mission on Earth card, the trickster becomes your guide. Outwitting your opponents by giving them a thing that really serves you is one of the necessary lessons to integrate. You must be like Br'er Rabbit, Anansi, and the Tricky Coyote to thrive. This lifetime will help you to develop your humor, your mental quickness, your will to win, and your ability to disguise yourself when necessary. This life path can also teach one how to evade capture by seeing options that others can't see.

Reverse

Follow the rules and the highest moral code that you have. Stepping to the bad side will work against you. Stay as sober as possible. Don't get caught in any drama. Don't cheat your way to your goal.

Practice

Crossroads—There is a choice that needs to be made. If you aren't sure what to do, just go to the crossroads near your home, hold three pennies to your head and then to your heart, and sincerely say, "Great Lord of the Crossroads, I see you testing my heart. Uncross my paths and you'll see me grow." It is at this point you will state your problem or what you need to get rid of in order to make your choice easier. Throw the three pennies into the middle of the crossroads and look away immediately. Do not look back.

Herbal Work

Saturnian plants are necessary to balance out craving and addictions. These plants are often bitter. The bitter flavor is sometimes needed to balance the body. Try drinking some gentian or dandelion root tea. A nonbitter Saturnian plant is elder. Drink some elder tea while being completely present in the body. Take note of the senses and how much more balanced you feel.

Tea: hibiscus, cinnamon, peppermint

16. THE TOWER—COSMIC BROKEN STUMP

Realm:	Planet:	Zodiac:	Herb:
5	Mars	Aries	cayenne

A tree has been destroyed by excessive force.

Sometimes the magic is in pushing and breaking. Bears push whole trees over, and harsh winds snap trees like twigs. Chicks crack the eggs they are in to emerge fresh and new. Smash through your shell and find the freshness inside. That which is truly sturdy in one season will remain sturdy in the next. All else will break.

Card Meanings

PUSH! PUSH! PUSH! Time is now!

Push only with your own might until you hear a snap! Be bold! Be proud! But also be ready for the lessons and also the pains that come with breaking. This card also warns of some kind of explosion that may happen around you soon, so get ready! Oftentimes it's a missile of life coming to blast at your own ego. This card also signifies abrupt endings, breakups, destruction of a structure, devastation, or complete demolition. Untimely or unnatural departures. This card mirrors the effects of acting too hastily or aggressively or proudly. Death to a thing as a result of trying to force growth or due to a lack of respect for natural cycles.

As your Mission on Earth, this card is asking you to time events based on your own inner time bomb. When you feel the explosion, it's time to act! There are times when you are going to need to bring the whole house down. You must be okay with seeing things explode in this lifetime. You will often be part of the demolition crew. Stand up to injustice and bring down systems that have oppressed your brothers and sisters! Break through barriers and shackles that have been placed on your mind. Destroy what the world does not need! Stand strong after it all comes crashing down, and yell, "Yes, I sure did! And I'd do it again!"

Reverse

Too much anger. Review your attraction to anger; you may be addicted. Your pride is a problem.

Practice

Grab three eggs. Hold each one for nine deep breaths while thinking of the breakthrough or the tough issue you need to face. If you have a cigar or a Natural American cigarette, start to smoke it while thinking of how big you are becoming. You are bigger than the issue at hand! Feeling fully charged up, yell "AH!!!" while throwing each egg to break at your feet. Now step over the yolks and go face your issue head-on.

Herbal Work

This is the time to work with Martian plants. Coffee has great abilities as a Martian plant that can get someone moving before or after a fight. Drink a cup while jotting down your Mission on Earth or an immediate mission. Time to get psyched up about why you are here. Dandelion or nettle tea can be a great herb for peeing out anger if anger is an obstacle.

Tea: nettle

17. THE STAR—THE INNOCENT

Realm:	Planet:	Zodiac:	Herb:
3	Uranus	Aquarius	cleavers

When we are born again, a new community often comes along with that. The new babes carry similarities. You are a fresh new baby being born into a fresh new world. You are a fresh sprout on firm ground. Lessons learned. Steer clear of what could bring down your vibration.

Card Meanings

Keep your vibration high, playful, private, and childlike. Play and make art and explore with the people who are like you, the ones that carry the same spark you were born with. These people will not judge you or take away from you. There are no expectations from them. Just existing in alignment with your own stars is placing you in the right place. Ignore those who have expectations for you; all you need to do is be. There is no planning or force in this space. There is only room for play and innocence and the laughter that comes with moving in spaces that are glad you exist.

If this pops up as your Mission on Earth, keep close to what is truly sacred. You must ask what is truly sacred, and walk with an open heart. This path is deeply personal, and it is not about fitting in. This path is about locating that sacred thing and expressing that.

Reverse

It's time to think about how others may feel about how you are living. Impressing others will bring rewards. Put on a show for the world. Stay true to your traditional fan base. Don't focus on yourself so much. It's time to work for the people.

Practice

Eggs are extremely yin and can pull away negative vibrations and implants. Rub an egg on your third eye for at least 5 to 15 minutes while taking deep, conscious breaths in order to pull away spiritual toxins. Set the egg under your bed for three days to continue to draw in negative energies that may need more time to be pulled in. After the three days, throw three pennies into a crossroads and leave the egg there.

Herbal Work

Cleavers, burdock, nettles, and other alterative plants are blood-cleansing and make the body feel fresh, allowing for the prana to move better through the body. Utilize plants like these to get toxins pushed out and to free up blocked prana.

Tea: burdock root

18. THE MOON—NOURISH

Realm:	Planet:	Zodiac:	Herb:
2	Moon	Cancer	marsh mallow

The seductive moon is affecting your thinking and movements. The trees are affected and, under the influence, feeling led to unzip from their tree shape to let loose their contents in honor of the brilliant night sky.

The effect of the moon on the tides is well known. Are you aware of your own inner tides? You are made of majority water. Have you been honoring the waters in your own body? Have you been drinking enough water?

Which parts of your personality are springing forth during this time? Are you aware of your various sides? Are you perceiving your emotions as a basis for absolute truth?

The moon changes faces. She is the master of all masks! Are you identifying too heavily with one? Are you referring only to your favorite mask as "I"?

Card Meanings

You were given many wonderful masks. Use them. Don't become entangled in one so much that you forget your versatility.

If this card is your Mission on Earth, you will need to work with lunar cycles. Honor each moon phase and align your actions with it. You are also the shape-shifter in the same way that the werewolf breaks free of its human form to merge with the night. You must shape-shift as your intuition sees fit. Your freedom is based on your ability to be who you need to authentically be in any given situation. This life path also asks that you honor secrets and secrecy.

Reverse

Speak from your heart and not from behind a mask.

Practice 1

Make a plan to go on a night walk. Your body is craving the night sky. Take a large drink of water and pour water while saying a prayer for the moon. Visualize yourself merging with her. Look up and see your own face in the moon's light shining right back at you.

Practice 2

Grab a Healing Tree branch during the day, and place the tree branch above your bed. Turn off the lights and imagine the branch (with living leaves still attached) unzipping and allowing its spiritual constituents to rain upon your spirit as you fall asleep. Sleep and pray under this tree branch every night branch until the leaves dry up.

Herbal Work

You need the Moon plants: sage, sagebrush, mugwort, and other plants that look like they've been kissed by moonlight. Either set the moon herb of your choice in the moonlight and burn it later, or set tea in the moonlight for at least an hour and drink it before the sun rises.

Tea: marsh mallow tea: Let the roots sit in water overnight in a reusable tea bag or cheesecloth. In the morning, squeeze the gooey mucilage out of the cheesecloth, and dunk the roots back into the water. Do this at least three times, and mix all the ooze into the water. Do not add heat to these roots.

19. THE SUN—RADIANCE

Realm:	Planet:	Zodiac:	Herb:
3	Sun	Leo	dandelion

The sun pins down trouble and shines brightly every day through being a master of habit, pattern, and rhythm. Rhythm is love. Consistency is creation. What you love will be visited over and over and be affected in a good way by your continued visitation. The sun is like that. He rises and sends warmth and then comes back to send more until he can give only a little. After giving a little light for a time, he can give more and more until he can give his highest level again. The blessing is that he is always there. His everyday habits keep things moving. The sun is telling you to watch your tendencies. What ideas do you allow in your head every day? How do you walk? What is your diet? Are you aware of how you affect people and your environment? Do you move through your life in ways that allow the light of the sun to shine through your eyes? Or do you live in a fantasy until things go wrong and then try to pray or perform magic, having ignored the patterns of your day-to-day life? The sun says that your day-to-day routines and habits *are* the magic you need to focus upon. This card can also be telling you that the answer you seek is right in your face. Go within, find the light, and it will shine on the seed you need to patiently grow.

If the sun is your Mission on Earth, you are a light to your world. Your family and friends should all be able to find joy in your presence. You should make it a point to relate to people so that you can share your light. Your mind is fast, and your generosity is boundless. These are great gifts. You are a royal and a bridge builder. Your life should be service-focused and rooted in helping people solve problems. Look to beings such as the Buddha and the Christ for inspiration. They are both incarnations of solar energy. Your light shines extremely bright! It would be wise to make sure you always have accountability around you. This is to keep you aware and properly moving through the effects of your negative traits. With so much light and energy pouring out of you, those negative traits may be hard to see at times. If your solar energy burns so bright that you get a following, stay in your virtue. Never go against the same code you taught your followers to respect. Remain humble while in your power. The voices in your head can start bending the rules so your heart can experience exciting yet truly dangerous terrain. The more light that pours out of you, the more you need to check in with someone to keep you reflective and grounded.

Card Meanings

There is no cheat code or savior for this situation other than in changing habits. Stretching, exercising, regular sunlight, high-magnesium foods, meditation, and qi-building techniques will add to you. Move with intention; and focus on moving in morality, good character, and paths proved to bring out your best! It would also be wise to completely let go of the victim mentality. Your birth never guaranteed your protection. There is no genie god that promised you'd never be hurt. The truth is that your links to divinity, your links to goodness and God, are all *earned* through the lessons you learn. This life is about acquiring wisdom windows that give you more and more access to divine light and multidimensional awakening. These windows are like building blocks that come together through understanding of the nine realms to help earn protection! Protection is not in gambling on a mystery god! Protection is passed down in healed families and/or collected throughout a lifetime. The good/God force can access you more and more through your ability to see his light through that fine collection of knowledge, wisdom, awareness, faith, and understanding. You will then meet others who also carry window blocks to add to yours. There's power there. The real power is not in begging a mystery savior god. Build up your own inner temple on solid principles, and the Great God will visit!

Reverse

Be sporadic. Live from the seat of your desires and cravings.

Practice

For nine days, pick a sunny space near a bunch of trees and salute the sun military-style. Pull out a journal and write your daily adventures and trials. Read through the entries you made for three consecutive Sundays; and on the last Sunday, name the the three entries as if they were a short book. Ask yourself, "What changes must the main character of my story make in order for the ending of this book to reflect my needs and wants?" Next time you pull the sun card, do the exercise again and compare the stories.

Herbal Work

Before the sun rises, grab seven sunflowers or St. John's wort and lay them facing the east. As the sun rises, talk or sing to the sun while pouring water onto the plants in front of you. Help the sun to rise! Once it is risen, thank the sun, make your declaration and speak many blessings over yourself. This will increase luck for three weeks and help with sad emotions.

Tea: dandelion root tea

solar tea: Allow solar herbs such as dandelion, sunflower, or yarrow to steep in the sun before drinking.

20. JUDGMENT—YHWH SHANGO

Realm:	Planet:	Zodiac:	Herb:
9	Mars	Aries	garlic

The ultimate war god, the judge, the highest single ruler, the I AM, the supreme, hot, expansive yang energy has appeared to you in a tree form. He requires you to follow strict rules during this time and to fear the consequences if you do not. He calmly tells you that you should fear your lord and provide the ultimate respect. If you are in alignment with your highest god, know that he will knock down anything standing in your way. Tell the Most High in your pantheon what is bothering you, and watch it blasted from view. Everything you are doing matters in this season. Move correctly and in alignment with the most aggressive and high god of your pantheon.

Card Meanings

It is what it is. The verdict is in! The fruits of your labor have come to maturity, and they have a story. A mixed bag of good and bad. It's time to see things as they really are and accept that life is messy. Don't hide behind the ego. Repent to those you have hurt, and accept what comes next. It is time for you to hear the truth and be accountable. Be disciplined, firm, honest, integral, and aggressive.

As a Mission on Earth, this path is one of extreme devotion to a cause. You are more than a conqueror. No weapon formed against your cause shall prosper. This is not a sit-around-and-wait card. This card is asking you to use what you see in front of you and make something amazing happen. Build something! Something strong. You can't lose in this life if you move in alignment with your Most High God. This is a card that could also be calling you toward the Hoodoo tradition in general. Pray near an oak tree or with oak leaves in your pocket. You need a strong and fully trusted father figure in this life to stretch you as he sees fit. This will pull you to new heights.

Reverse

Take it easy; there may be a different outcome. Do a reading or try doing some ritual work or magical things to change the outcome.

Practice

Take your Bible, Quran, a Shango Odu, or a story of your most powerful chief god, and read a random page under an oak tree while keeping your goal in mind. What does that scripture you read say about your challenge? If you can, choose to fast from food for three consecutive Thursdays or Sundays.

Herbal Work

Start a full campfire in your backyard or simply light a candle. Stare into those flames and focus. Feel the big fire burning within. If you want to roar, go ahead and roar. If you need to pray or read a scripture, do that. Take rosemary or garlic or another herb known for its spiritually cleansing properties and gently rub them in your hands. Intentionally, sprinkle them into the fire. Say a prayer while focusing on your intentions and then take nine pictures of the flames. Analyze the shapes that pop out in the photos and write what they could mean for you.

Tea: cacao

21. THE WORLD—A NEW UNDERSTANDING

Realm:	Planet:	Zodiac:	Herb:
8	Saturn	Capricorn	bay leaf

The woman closed her eyes and saw the entire world inside. She wept because she finally saw things in their totality and could see her natural role in it.

Card Meanings

There are limits to what each of us can and should do. Those limits are the source of freedom. The limits are freeing because of the realization that one doesn't have to be everything to everyone. You are part of something big. Learn your place if you don't know it. If you've learned your part, then play it well and don't step into someone else's role.

This card can also indicate that something is complete. There are times when one may want to know if they are in the right place or if the team has all the right pieces. If this card pops up on a question, there is nothing else to add. This card is a cap. The pieces are there. Play your part and ensure success.

The goal of your life if this card pops up as your Mission on Earth is to build community through honoring your limitations. You need a solid team. This life is about you doing the inner work so the team that you need most manifests on the outside of you. This team is an extension of yourself.

Reverse

Do your own thing. Do not consider the whole.

Practice

Go to a place with trees. Gather one leaf from any five trees and write one thing you are grateful for on each one. Place these five leaves under your pillow for three nights and write down your dreams in the morning. On the third day, take the leaves and place them on a house altar, or bury them if the dreams were unpleasant.

Herbal Work

Get some bay leaves and make tea from them. Visualize the plant spirit of bay rising from within your own heart. Meditate and feel that medicine moving through you. Hear what bay has to say, even if it's only one word that comes to you. Intuit that message out loud. It could be helpful to have someone close by to record the messages for you.

Tea: bay leaf

22. OSAIN—THE HEALING SHRINE

Realm:	Planet:	Zodiac:	Herb:
1	Moon	Cancer	Baobab

The poor man had lost one arm, one leg, one ear, and one eye, but he found a way to stand anyway. He took a step and his missing leg became a tree. He reached for a flower with the arm that wasn't there, and his arm was a tree branch. It reached the flower just fine. When he opened the eye that wasn't upon his face, he realized that he could see through the pores and scars of the trees; and when he listened, he could hear with the ears of the birds above. In his injury, he had become more whole than he was before.

Card Meanings

Your healing will come with the assistance of nature spirits, healing herbs, or looking at your own inner shadow. There are parts of you that are starving. There are also agreements that must be kept in order to remain healthy. This is in regard to the body, mind, and spirit. This card warns that pacts must be honored even if they feel uncomfortable or limiting. Unfortunately, there are those of us who make commitments not really knowing how to honor them. If you are picking this card, it's important that you seek counsel, get divination, and do many things until you figure it out. If you are having a health issue, you need to honor what you put into your body. If your family is upset with you now, the fault is not theirs. There is an agreement you are not honoring. Be humble and figure it out. Even if you are being haunted by a shrine or a ghost or a nightmare, this card indicates that the problem is you. You have not fully honored your side of the agreement. If you think you've given enough, you are either wrong or giving the wrong form of payment. You must make the proper sacrifice either internally or externally so that harmony is restored.

During this phase, lean on Nighttime Object helpers such as roots or leaves attached to tree branches. Bring them into the home and pray with them. There is medicine in the shadow of the rue plant and many others as well. This card is also about collecting talismans and building proper relationships with the angelic shadows of the self and the plant world. This card could also be asking you to bring a plant into your home or to plant a tree in your backyard.

If you pull this card as your Mission on Earth, you are the **Rootworker**. Work the roots, pull out the beauty that hides in the shadows of yourself, and don't hide from your destiny.

Reverse
Too much dependency on charms and external helper spirits.

Practice
Sit in complete darkness with a plant of choice and listen for nine consecutive nights. If you hear a message, write it down. If not, pray for the health of the plant after the meditation ends.

Herbal Work

Take leaves from nine plants and add them to cool water. Pour some rum into the water and say a prayer. Gently place your hands in the water, and rip the plants to pieces while praying. Pray for whatever you need, and then use your hands to rub that water all over you from head to toe.

Tea: ashwagandha, burdock, and cinnamon root

23. JIRIDON—THE TREE WHISPERER

Realm:	Planet:	Zodiac:	Herb:
4	Moon	Cancer	chamomile

The strange girl said, "If you don't tell the trees your secrets, why should they tell you theirs?" She proceeded to whisper into the leaf, and the whole tree shook as winds blew that were not present before.

Card Meanings

This is not the time to tell everyone about what you are working on in private. You should minimize talking to humans. If you must talk about this thing, maybe tell one person. This is a time of not talking to people. Perhaps your idea is too sensitive to survive the slightest negative thought from another; perhaps the universe wants you to go through a sponge phase of absorption. Either way, now is not the time to be out and proud and judgmental and boisterous.

In a Mission on Earth Spread, this card indicates the **Plant Healer**. It's important that you work with the plants, whisper to them, and take them into dream space with you. When you are in full alignment with who you really are, you'll find your green thumb, and the voices from the plants will be in your ears. In this life, act in a thoughtful way and find moments of long silence before you speak. This lifetime is about hearing. Seek to understand before seeking to be understood.

Reverse

Tell everyone what is on your heart.

Practice

Walk to a tree and tell that tree what it is you are working on and any other deep secrets you wish to share. Whisper directly into the node of the branch, the trunk, or the leaves. When the wind hits you or if you feel a slight change in temperature or mood, your subtle body has received its medicine and its answer. Take nine deep breaths and depart. Visit this tree often and treat it as a friend in general.

Herbal Work

Drink chamomile or any moon herb right before bed for nine consecutive nights. Take note of what dreams come to you while sleeping. Take note of your daydreams as well. If you don't recall any of your dreams or daydreams, do another nine days without smoking or eating white sugar, red meat, catfish, or pork.

Tea: 1 part anise, 3 parts chamomile flowers, 1 part peppermint

24. BEAR TREE—THE WALKING TREE ORACLE

Realm:	Planet:	Zodiac:	Herb:
9	Earth	all	aspen

The tree saw the bear and became a bear made of wood and leaves. The people saw this strange moving tree animal and asked it what kind of witchcraft made it move like a living animal. The Walking Tree spoke and the people kneeled, for it was neither bear nor tree but an oracle. A sure gift from the deepest areas of time-space.

Card Meanings

Bear Tree is the Walking Tree calling upon you to stand in your integrity and walk the walk. This card also requires that you openly protect what you love. This is an action card. This is a card of steady movement and power. The meditation must not stop when you come out of your meditation. When you stand from your sitting and reflecting, you must continue in that spirit and walk in it.

Meditation can no longer be used as a relaxing escape; it must become part of your mundane life. You must bridge both worlds in the same way that the bear bridges worlds by walking on all fours like an animal and standing on two legs like a human. In the same way that bear was able to lead humans to healing herbs and medicines, your awareness will bring what is best for you.

If Bear Tree is your Mission on Earth, it's time to be the blessing that you want to see in the world. You must be the sage and the guru and move in authority, knowing that no one will do it for you. This is a card of service to the planet! You must protect life, because every living being on the planet is a living life-giving portal. When an animal or plant goes extinct, a door disappears and there is no way to bring it back. If this is your incarnation card, you are a **Tree Walker**. Incarnated in this lifetime as an answer to Earth's call for its own strongest healers, Tree Walkers are the ones who must master the self in order to walk with a strong inner stillness. Work closely with your power animal and think with your guts! Don't try to take on everything at once. Remember, you must always be working to have stillness inside as your foundation.

Reverse

You must detach from the world to find your peace. Escape and pursue your ideals. Travel. Your peace is not in the vicinity.

Practice

Light your candles and sit in a meditation posture for at least 9 minutes. Picture yourself in a safe place. Imagine your true lair, a place holding all the things you need to feel safe and natural. An animal will enter the room. That is your power animal. Feed your animal and then merge with the animal. Open your eyes, and walk the rest of the day in this state of perfect balance with your true nature.

Herbal Work

Drink a tea of strong roots, and pour some of the tea into a small hole. Pray over the hole while blowing your breath and/or tobacco smoke into the hole, and then cover it up. The prayer is now planted. Watch the prayer grow and grow over the next nine months.

Tea: yellow dock root

25. ANCESTORS—MY WAYS

Realm:	Planet:	Zodiac:	Herb:
7	Pluto	Scorpio	impepho

The altar is set. The candle has been lit. The ancestors are led to the fire. It appears like a strange new sun in their world, pulling them in. Many have already shown up. People you knew while they were living. People who wish the best for you. People who know your ways.

Card Meanings

Your ancestors are deciding to speak through coincidences and through your family. Do not ignore what they are telling you. Pay attention to the people, colors, opportunities, animals, and music that come your way. If that music stirs your soul, the ancestors sent it as a gift. Be grateful to them. Pour water for them and offer foods that have always reached the core of your bones. If a specific ancestor is popping up, give them what they enjoyed while they were living. You can light a candle and read a favorite scripture, offer a can of soda, or even play a specific song.

Honor the elders in your family. Are you neglecting an important elder who needs your assistance? That elder will be on the other side one day. If that elder was someone good to you before they lost their mobility or lost their mind, it is wise to still find ways to serve them even if it has to be indirect. If they lead good lives, they will be restored on the other side and will be good to those who honored them in their time of hardship. This card can often speak of a blessing that is coming through the bloodline.

If this card is your Mission on Earth, you are the **Ancestral Shaman**. You are here to go deep into the esoteric and medicinal ways of your direct ancestors. Life will ask you to pull out the rituals, tools, prayers, and herbs that will benefit your own healing. You are then asked to share what you can with your family, friends, and community. Sometimes the family isn't ready for the full package, so give what you can. Be mindful of this task, and honor the boundaries of those causing their own suffering. There is no need to get angry or seclude yourself, even though there are times you'll want to do both.

Reverse

No need to do ancestor work right now. They are satisfied with you. A young person may need a helping hand. Reverse may also warn of a dysfunctional ancestor who is too close to you. Set up an altar, and call higher guides to set boundaries.

Practice

Light a candle and leave some food out for your most elevated and evolved ancestors for nine consecutive nights to give them a power boost. Call their names while spraying rum or whiskey in all four directions. This is necessary for the work they want to do for you. If you have a drum or a cooking pot, beat the drum for them to get them dancing and vibing with you. If you have time, tell them about what's been going on in your life while eating as well. Listen for any joyful or enlightening thoughts.

Herbal Work

Grab some marigold flowers, which are known in some parts of the world as a flower that ancestral spirits can easily sense from the other side. Place these around a candle at night, and sing songs that pleased your grandparents or great-grandparents on either side of the family.

Tea: cinnamon

26. MOTHER OF GOD—THE CALLING

Realm:	Planet:	Zodiac:	Herb:
9	Venus	Taurus	linden

The maiden frolics in the field, not knowing that she will be spoken of throughout the ages. Her offspring is the light of the world. She is the only one who can give the ultimate formless yang force a physical form. She is the embodiment of form and coolness and a love that can come only from women. Through her yin, the yang can be balanced, and something perfect can be created. Without yin, yang can only be a destroyer of worlds.

Card Meanings

If you pull this card, know that destiny has chosen you in this moment. You are dancing right to the fruits of your born purpose. This time may not be met with big appreciation from big audiences or huge acclaim, but you are in your authenticity, and someone is taking notes and watching you make moves that will affect up to seven generations from now. None of the people in the holy books knew they were in holy books. You are one of those folks.

This is a "Yes!" card telling you to keep going in the current direction. You are about to birth something major, even if you can't sense that. Move in faith. The evidence may not be apparent for many years, but you are covered and protected and called to be what you were designed to be. You are a vessel for a greatness that only you can give birth to. As great and creative as the universe is, it still needs you to birth its will on the earth. A god with no earth is a god with no birth. You are the birther. Don't hide from your calling.

If this is the card that your Mission on Earth has brought you to, you are the **Anointed One**. You've incarnated many times and have learned some of the hardest lessons. This has made you strong and very spiritually protected. Your medicine is in reading the signs and birthing the messages sent from the divine. Flow with the spirit properly, and birth what is placed upon your heart. This path can cause some people to want to support and love everyone. Be careful of supporting those who have only caused you harm. Be mindful; your aura is extremely attractive, so you'll need to use discernment around why each person is coming to you. Many will think the power they feel through their attraction to you is a sign that you are their soulmate. This is not true. This is just a normal reaction of people who can sense what you are. Your Mission on Earth forbids you from consuming the vibrations that lie in pigs or catfish. Steer clear of consuming large amounts of alcohol and inhaling too much smoke from burning marijuana.

Reverse
You are in the wrong story. It is not worth pursuing. Your beautiful garden is elsewhere.

Practice
Grab a quartz crystal, close your eyes, and rub the quartz gently upon your third eye to clear any spiritual clutter from upon you. When you feel as if the quartz has cleared away any undesirable energies from that area, hold that quartz in your left hand and allow it to continue pulling. Feel yourself being pulled into the quartz and baptized in golden or white light. When you feel renewed, open your eyes. Cleanse the quartz in salt overnight. An egg can also be used here instead of quartz, but pray over the egg and discard it near or in a river or spring before three days is up.

Herbal Work
Light a Virgin de Guadalupe candle or an Oshun candle or a Yemaya candle or a blue candle, burn copal or sage and add some rose petals to a cup of water, and place your hands over your ovaries. It doesn't matter if you are male or female. Focus on your womb. Meditate on your mother and your own ability to birth what you need in this world.

Tea: bee balm

Realm:	Planet:	Zodiac:	Herb:
1	Pluto	Scorpio	cannabis

The Ghost Tree takes in the wails of the dead, pulling in the grief, sadness, and the awful fears that haunt the humans. The Ghost Tree is a palace for the hungry and a place of rest for the distorted. The benevolent find no solace here, and only the wretched have a chance.

Card Meanings

The Ghost Tree is not where you want to be, because the cost is too high. You do not have the self-reflection skills, the maturity, the right timing, the knowledge, the power, or the right resources to handle this. Move the other way. No life can come from it unless you wish to be haunted or pay for some time. It is most often wise to let this thing go. Take another path until you are stronger. This card warns of true deep-seated bad luck stemming from moving further. You may not wish to deal with the curses that come from moving alongside this. This card warns that the path you wish to take is forbidden and too expensive in the long run. That what you get out is not equal to what you'll have to give to receive something good. There's an imbalance. This is a weak point in your story to avoid. It is best to leave this door unopened unless you wish to be pulled into misery that may not be worth the work. This is a card warning of a trap or foul play. Your honest actions may be summoning your worst enemy. Be mindful of the huge trap you are laying for yourself. This card can warn of energy vampires, chronic disease, or poisoning as well. This tree is a big black stop sign. Think hard about how much time you have if you wish to proceed. Do you love a thing enough to be food for it? This card can also warn of cursed items that should be removed from the house. A great time for a reading from a skilled diviner.

This card can warn about the dangers of hoarding and selfishness. Being too attached to physical possessions. Possessions may own you. This card mainly speaks of haunted objects or other hungry ghosts. Many modern store-bought plastic Barbie-type dolls, porcelain dolls, and ceramic statues are in fact leeching beings that are easy containers for starving vampiric beings. If you get this card, you might need to either feed or get rid of something in the home or even toxins in the body.

If this card is pulled as part of a Mission on Earth, you are the **Redeemer**! You incarnated to face off against the generational curses handed down in the family. A Redeemer must be fearless and humble as they go into the shadows to shed light on all the junk that needs to be burned away. The Redeemer is often called to work with those who are addicts, unhoused, imprisoned, or completely outcast by society due to unacceptable behaviors, offenses, or occupations. The Redeemer is an extremely powerful path that allows one to look deeply into their own fears so that they can guide others. Redeemers know who they can help, based on where they have been. Their past misery is a sure sign of where their ministry must go. Some Redeemers make great prophets, because they understand both evil and their own shadow so well that goodness and love emit from all aspects of their lives.

Other Redeemers are very effective at using magic as a form of revenge. They will be very much attracted to hexing and cursing and should know about these things in order to know how to defend against these attacks.

All Redeemers must beware of addictive patterns in life and the possibility of being consumed by the power that is promised to them by demonic entities.

Reverse

Health and healing are within grabbing distance. No need to stress too hard over the issue at hand. The problem will be ending quickly.

Practice

Take a tent to a camping spot or a backyard, say a prayer, and spend the whole night out there. Sacrificing your bed for a night will be a major statement to your guides.

Herbal Work

Take rum or whiskey, hibiscus tea or root beer, to a nearby tree. Put some of the beverage into the mouth, and spray the base of the tree nine times. Fall to your knees and tell the tree what you're trying to rid yourself of. Take three leaves home with you and wear them on your person for nine days.

Trees: sycamore, purple European beech, willow, she oak, breadfruit

Tea: marijuana, hops

28. HEALING TREE—PLAY AND PEACE

Realm:	Planet:	Zodiac:	Herb:
6	Venus	Libra	juniper

The Healing Tree is surrounded by the friendly fairies, playful pixies, and laughing, lighthearted spirits.

Card Meanings

If you pull this card, it's time to move from a heart space. A revelation will come to you soon around a type of love. Pay attention to your relationships. You may learn about how to have proper boundaries around love; you may see a sign to let your guard down. You may be on the verge of finding a lover or a life partner or moving into a comfortable relationship with local nature spirits. Be open to whatever this heart message is. This is a good luck card and a blessing for those who pull it. If you need further clarity after pulling this card, feel free to pull another to steer you in the right direction.

If this card represents your Mission on Earth, you are the **Magical Child**. You are pleasant, have deep love for people, and have many magical insights to share. You are here to help people to remember what soul parts they lost in their childhood. Your presence and example can help these lost soul parts find their way back home. You are the sweetness of life. People love to be around you and can sense the many fairies and helper spirits you bring into a room. Just like the Healing Trees, you project so many good vibes into the atmosphere. **Warning**: Be careful of being too trusting and open. You have the ability to see the best in others, but there are those that wish to make a meal out of you.

Reverse

There is no time for comfort or play. It is time to buckle down and do the hard work.

Practice

Wear a costume, mask, or hooded robe to the Healing Tree of your choice and find a stick lying nearby. Pick this stick up and declare it to be your wand. Point this wand at the tree and tell the tree spirits that you have arrived. Once you sense them, kneel and tell them you are ready to be healed. They will begin to dance around you. As the sensation around you grows, be sure to join in or at least clap and sing for them. If people begin to watch, just continue anyway. If this would be too embarrassing, participate in your mind (Realm 5). Be sure to use your imagination with this practice until you can sense these beings clearly in Realm 6.

Herbal Work

Hang St. John's wort, juniper, hawthorn, or a strong Healing Tree branch at the entrance to your door. Open the door and invite the sunlight and the benevolent fairy energies to enter the home. Mix 9 drops of lemon, rosemary, and peppermint essential oil in a bucket of water. Add a shot of rum to the water. Stir, then wash the floor from the back of your home to the front of your home.

Trees: juniper, aspen, hawthorn, ash, cottonwood, baobab, guava

Tea: juniper berries

29. COMMANDER TREE—DELEGATION

Realm:	Planet:	Zodiac:	Herb:
5	Mars	Aries	pine leaf

The Commander Tree stands strong as the plant king of the forest!

Card Meanings

If you pull this card, it's time to stand strong and take charge! The idea here is to be aggressive and execute the plan. Anytime you are pulling one of the tree cards, it implies that you could use actual tree spirit cooperation. In this case, you want to work with Commander Trees. There will also be messages coming about fighting styles, strategy, or managing hot emotions. Be open to what comes within a nine-day period.

If this card is your Mission on Earth, know that you are the **Fighter**! Your mission is to never run in the face of adversity. You will show others what true courage looks like through facing every fear head-on. There is no monster to run from. There is no dragon to fear. Your mission is to grow your own inner dragon until it becomes sturdy and strong enough for you to protect what you love. This card has a huge warning about cowardice. The more you run from a threat, the stronger it shall become. So embrace your inner fighter, strategize, and then execute!

Reverse

Play the supportive role. Do not take charge!

Practice

Light a red candle and write down all that you wish to be rid of in your life. Meditate on the burning of that page and all the evils that come with it. When you open your eyes, take the paper to running water and set it ablaze. Throw the ashes into the river.

Herbal Work

Find a tree that is an oak, or a pine, or a tree that you believe to have Commander qualities. Or you can go to a tree that has some lightning-god-style folklore tied to it. Add nine leaves to your pockets or put them in a neck sachet, and visualize an assertive version of you getting the result that you want. After you have visualized, write the plan and take action.

Trees: pine, white oak, red oak, sandbox, sea grape

Tea: ginger

30. GURU TREE—GREAT MYSTERY

Realm:	Planet:	Zodiac:	Herb:
9	Saturn	Aquarius	mugwort

The Guru Tree is tugging on the boundaries of your consciousness. The great green unknown pushes you to periodically lose your sense of humanness. Who are you without it? What are you? The terrain is challenging, and the Guru Tree does not aim to bring comfort.

Card Meanings

If you pull this card, know that comforts may be moved away in order for mind expansion. A challenge is on the way. This card is not a card of rest and ease. It's quite the opposite. Your boundaries, the ones you built to keep you safe, will be tested. You may be forced to loosen them in one area and tighten them in another. This is the tree of uncomfortable expanse, and these trees push until you get the lesson. Humility, patience, and deep breathing will be necessary as you birth a new perspective, a new type of awareness, and a deepened understanding of multidimensionality. This tree type can be looked at as containing the energy that pulled in so tight that an explosion occurred. A slingshot pulls back before it shoots an object outward.

If you have received this card as your Mission on Earth, you are learning to be the **Master Teacher**. You are here to make the knowers uncomfortable and push them into deeper truths! The key in this path is to always remember compassion. Develop the sensitivity to know when you are pushing too hard. This can be hard to do when your foresight is super clear and you are watching the people around you make so many mistakes. The message here is that there is a wrong way to be right! You must use tact in working with others. This mission is also very green. This means that working with Guru Trees and studying the mysteries of nature are extremely important. You must also work with the elderly. This will bring many blessings your way.

Reverse

There's no need to bend your mind too much over this issue. Play it safe and stick to what is familiar.

Practice

Walk to a nearby park and choose a tree to be your personal Guru Tree. Kneel before the tree and ask the tree to reveal itself to you. Walk nine steps away from the tree, and focus on the tree for no less than an hour. Take notes on what you see. Do this for nine consecutive days or nine consecutive Sundays. The tree must begin to trust you to open up to you, so don't fret if it takes a while to see.

Herbal Work

Choose maple leaves, elm leaves, or leaves from a tree you've been intuitively led to as your own guru leaves, and tell the spirit that you are ready for the expansion. Tell the spirit you are ready for the change even if it is uncomfortable. Place the leaves on your altar underneath a seven-day candle. Burn myrrh resin while praying a protection prayer from your base spiritual tradition or reciting the Psalms. Light the candle to activate the next phase, and let it burn all the way down.

Trees: maple, elm, Mohagany

Tea: mugwort

Realm:	Planet:	Zodiac:	Herb:
5	Venus	Taurus	Ispilanthes

There's a man standing alone under a tree. His thoughts are wrapped completely in himself.

Card Meanings

There's a time for everything. Right now it's time to stop. Don't plan, don't talk, don't even entertain the possibilities. It's time for a check-in. What are your true deepest needs, and how is this situation not honoring those needs? There are times when a person is possessed by an inner dream that leads only to more and more confusion and pain. It's triggered when things seem good and safe. The question is: How does the dream take over? The answer is impulsivity and blind spots. You can't see outside of the dream. You can only feed it and suffer from its consequences. It is time to stop and pray and call your mentor, your pastor, your parents, or anyone who can slow you down and hold you accountable.

If you pull this card as your Mission on Earth, you are a **Soul Guardian**. You are here to coach people on how to practice patience and wisdom and how to slow down in times of great change or emotional extremes. It is during strange times that one must listen to their soul and be held accountable by an outside force. Sometimes the storms within are so strong we need help to remain tethered to who we are. There are times when the stranger is yourself! As a Soul Guardian, you must stay rooted in who you are so that you can coach those who come to you. Don't ever get so wrapped up in a project or person that you lose your tether to your own soul. There will be times when you also need to stop. With Venus being present in this card, I highly warn against being too nice to the people you are trying to coach, parent, or protect.

Reverse

Get busy! What are you waiting for?

Practice

Skip breakfast, lunch or dinner and walk or drive to a far secluded spot and sit until time for the next meal. or for serious issue, eat no solid foods for the entire day.

Herbal Work

What do you wish to let go of? Write it on paper and wrap that paper in Spanish moss or bindweed. Throw it in a river or bury it in a secret location.

Tea: spearmint and honey

32. THE UNICORN—MAGICAL HELP

Realm:	Planet:	Zodiac:	Herb:
9	Neptune	Pisces	passionflower

A unicorn has come to aid a faithful maiden.

Card Meanings

The helper spirits have heard the call. Tune into them! They are with you. Miracles are afoot! Your good karma has returned to you. Shift perspective so you can witness the miracle. If you have pulled this card, you are in the presence of saints, angels, magical creatures, and heart-centered savior beings. Activate these beings. Cooperate with them. This is not the time to draw solely from your inner power. You need a magical crutch for now. Your familiars, power animals, and plant guardians are strong! Tell them what you need them to do! This is also a card that may indicate a visitation from your future self. Blessing recognition is a very important skill to develop so that you can recognize what is before you. If you can't recognize the treasures, helpers, and opportunities that your guides set before you, you won't receive them.

If this card is popping up as your Mission on Earth, you are a **Summoner**! Your voice has the tones to attract and summon some of the most powerful, ancient, and miracle-working spirits! They recognize all the work you did with them in your previous incarnations, and so they will show up for you. Be careful to balance this gift. Spirits also have lives of their own and can't always show up to perform a big miracle. Sometimes you will be called to be your own miracle. It is imperative that you are kind to strangers. Some of them are horses for angelic beings testing your heart. In other words, when that "regular" stranger catches you off guard while you are busy and asks for help, remember that a divine being is in their auric field watching you. This test can also come in the form of a strange call for help from a family member or friend. If you are pulling this card, you must help. One reason that helper spirits are attracted to you right now is that you are being called to be a helper spirit for someone now.

A Summoner Mission on Earth is not easy due to all its themes that revolve around illusion and deep emotion. Your spirits must be called upon to get through it. Ask for what you need, but also be mindful of what you ask for and who you call upon! They will show up! In your dealings with people, always ask for help when you need it, but don't ask for help from those who can't deliver.

Reverse

There's no one coming to save you. Utilize what you know, and formulate a practical plan of action. Pull from your own personal power. You are everything you need.

Practice

You are surrounded by amazing beings, and it's time to see them. Take a water bottle, pencil, and pad to a nearby tree. Stand under the tree and say, "Most beautiful creatures … helpers! Known and unknown! (pour water) I know you are here! (pour water) In the name of all that is sound and good for my life path, I grant you permission to intervene! (pour water)" Sit with the pencil and pad, and sketch yourself and all the helpers around you. Who do you imagine has come to answer your call? Set that drawing on the altar of your home.

Herbal Work

Take time to go to a natural space and grab several beautiful flowers, sticks, rocks, and nice-smelling herbs. While in a meditative state of mind, use what was collected to create a beautiful pattern on the floor of the natural setting. Light four candles honoring the four directions, burn copal or frankincense, and pray for what you wish!

Tea: ashwagandha and burdock root

33. SANKOFA—LOOK BACK

Realm:	Planet:	Zodiac:	Herb:
7	Saturn	Aquarius	tamarind

There's a tree looking over the waters. The native people who were with the tree in the beginning were taken. In despair, he fashions himself to appear in their likeness. Now he resembles those he loves so much. He stares into the waters, remembering them and praying for their safe return.

Card Meanings

There is a treasure, or a lesson, or an opportunity in your past. It is time to go back and fetch it! Look through old photos, look at old writings, and don't ignore any signs that come leading you backward in time.

In the beginning there was a fool, and in the end there was a griot. If this card is your Mission on Earth, you are a **Griot**, a keeper of stories. You are the one to weave the stories together in ways that inspire your clan. Live out the wisdom in the stories you learn by making the tough decisions. It is also imperative for you to pay attention to the patterns that pop up in your life. All of these patterns help to guide your storytelling. Stories are patterns. Observation, knowing, and storytelling should all be developed. Storytelling is your big medicine. Beware of using your gift to spread gossip and judgment. Beware of gossip-loving people.

Reverse

Do not speak about the past. Let it go and forge a new path!

Practice

Pour water first in honor of your enlightened ancestors. Then pray for the healing of all the rest. Pray as if you are giving a sermon to an entire church. Really get into it. Pour water for your lost soul parts. Say: "I call back all necessary parts of me that have been forced to leave me." Close your eyes and meditate and imagine all your soul parts coming back to you. Imagine them singing the most beautiful spiritual music as they begin to come home.

Herbal Work

On a piece of paper, write down everything you have lost and want back. This includes parts of yourself and things that you used to do. Pray a prayer that was meaningful to your ancestors while ripping the paper into small bits. Mix the ripped paper in a bowl with bits of fresh orange peel, mint, and dandelion flowers. Place a candle in the middle of the bowl. Light the candle while taking nine deep breaths and then recite, "I call back all necessary parts of me that have been forced to leave me." Let the candle burn. When the candle burns out, leave the remaining parts at the point where two roads meet or in a trash can at a place of worship.

Tea: hibiscus, clove, ginger, and cinnamon

THE ROYAL COURT

Every time we open a book, tell a story, or lay down an oracular spread, we are peering into a window of potentiality while also calling that reality closer to our own.

Everything is real in the multiverse. If you can perceive it, it exists. The Royal Court cards in this deck call to your place in New Africa. In Nu Africa there are rightful and just kings and queens who have counsels of wise elders, vast armies, beautiful languages, cities, and everything that you'd want or need. There are many clans, and each one falls within the resonance of one of the four elements: earth, air, fire, and water.

OVERVIEW

Kings

The Kings all represent the *north* direction—Obatala (yin stability), who made Earth habitable by sprinkling baobab powder on the waters. Obatala is slow and wise and brought a chicken to help spread earth so earth beings could walk about. Obatala made humans from clay soil. Asé. Slow, sound judgment and a sturdy foundation. The elder. The ways of old folks. The one who manifests as solid and unmoved.

Kings are the expertise of planning, protections, boundaries, and mental power (mind). The King is solid, patient, and mature and seeks to understand before being understood. He asks many questions, knowing that power is not in seeking validation. When shaken, the King seeks counsel from wise Kings in his network. The King's charge to perform his tasks is energized by the passionate Queen and inspired by the young and beautiful Princess. The

King is the guard and the ruler of interactions that may spawn from outside forces.

King spiritual tools are shrines and herbs, and roots and holy branches with leaves attached.

Queens

The Queens all represent the *south* direction—Oya (yang movement), who dances in the winds that spread the raging fires. The warrior Queen and mother of nine wears a beard when racing into battle. She, Oya, is also the hustle and bustle of the busy marketplace and the remarkable saleswoman. Asé. Fast choices led by an inner knowing or resonance. Gut feelings, psychic visions, drums leading to trances, and nights full of wild dreams. Queens are the want for more, the chase, the dance, the movement, and changes that come with bravely facing emotional highs and lows. The Queen is the appreciation of and the desire to consume physical things and seek physical pleasures.

Queens are the action masters who can buckle down and create what is necessary due to the King's protection and boundary-keeping. The King creates a safe foundation that unlocks her intense orgasms while also providing a blueprint for what should be birthed. She gives birth to new life through burning away the old and worn out. The Queen is the work and range of emotions that come with having a life filled with purpose and responsibilities. She remembers when a King found her. She was once a

Princess until impregnated with fire. Though supported by the King, the Queen is inspired by the adventurous Prince (whom she birthed), who will take her magic into the world and ultimately become a cool and wise King himself.

Queen spiritual tools are candles, the sun, and cooked herbs or food offerings.

Knighted Princes

The Knighted Princes all represent the *east* direction—Shango (yang spreading), master of the skies and beater of the drum. Shango is the lightning, the flashy one full of dazzling tricks and charisma and always with an impressive entourage. He is the loudest one in the room and the most effective debater. He loves to win and enjoys all sports and competitions. He is also the skilled hunter, going deep into the dark places to bring meat to the King's table.

The Princes are like quickly moving winds, the spreading of information, media, control of masses, cultural pride, or nationalism. The full ability to consume. The adult. The sky road for the traveling sun. Princes are the world-stage performers and true spreaders of the work as the programmed speaker for the King and Queen. The Prince exists to spread their will through mass movements and propaganda. He doesn't question their orders and seeks pleasure in accomplishing each new mission well. Strange new ideas that come from the open-minded Princesses he runs into along the way will spark him to consider other ways of moving in the world. He represents action and travel and pushing to the extreme of a thing.

The Prince tools are prayer and holy book readings dedicated to warlike creator gods; and breathing and smudging.

Priestess Princesses

The Priestess Princesses all represent the *west* direction— Osun (yin reflecting), the beautiful meadow. Osun is the woman in the field giggling, singing, and talking to her own reflection in a mirror or slow-moving stream. The lovely Osun was satisfied with having no responsibilities. People around the kingdom would give Osun various tasks, but Osun was scolded by them for taking her time and doing nothing they considered useful, so they prayed that she be taken away. Their wish was granted. They rejoiced until they realized that no crops grew in the land and no sex could happen; therefore, no woman could conceive. They prayed for her return; and when she came back, women could conceive and crops could grow. The Princess teaches us that rest and play are mandatory for health and well-being. She teaches that taking life too seriously can cause illness and that it's okay to let someone else do the work sometimes. She asks us to take a step back and wonder if the work was even truly ours to begin with.

The Princess is the element of life. She represents the juiciest fruits. She is a reflection and romance. Rest. Intuiting the spirits. Being an open vessel for the filling of the spirit. The Princess is a fully open vessel who is open to new spirits. The Princess is the spark, the inspiration, and the idea. She hopes to meet a lover who can honor her need to be free. The deep truth about the Princess is that she wants to feel free. She peacefully rests on all the work put in by the other members of the kingdom. Due to the trinity of King/Queen/Prince, she can rest on that triangle and dream. The King observes and plans, the Queen works hard to birth what is in her soul, while the Prince prepares for a trip. Everything is accounted for, which gives the Princess time to play and imagine whatever she wants.

The Princess tools are libation, being with water, and sound healing.

THE ROYAL COURT CARDS UNLOCKED

Earth Kingdom

The Earth Kingdom is the land in the highest mountains up north. It is the coolest and most grounded of the lands, known for its mineral-rich soils and vast wealth. Legend has it that the Earth Kingdom ancestors were the people of the stars who came down to shape the earth to make it habitable for all of the humans and land beings. The Earth Kingdom holds the precious memories of the realm in the griots who walk about. These storytellers hold the oral traditions that have carefully been passed from generation to generation. The griots are also priests who can channel the messages of the impeccable stones. All around the kingdom the stones are arranged in clumps and blessed with blood. They become living shrines that protect the land from spiritual invasion and keep everyone grounded and focused without distraction.

I. King of Earth

You can only be as rich as your financial literacy. The King of Earth is a financial and health planner. This is the richest Royal Court card in the deck. This card is asking you to sit and learn and become grounded in your eating and financial patterns.

Card Meanings

Analyze data, meet with an accountant, do not move without sound planning, check your inventory, get a health checkup, examine your diet, manage your household without emotional highs and lows. This card's advice is that you should have more and that you can have more but you may have holes in your system that need to be filled.

This card refers often to a male (or anyone with hard-to-ignore masculine qualities, energy, or styles of dress) with a solid foundation. His home is full of high-quality assets and comfortable furniture. His bills are all paid, and his finances are completely in order. He takes care of his things and can spend hours cleaning his car or admiring the fruits of his labor. He may be a lazy man who uses his cleverness to get what he desires. He may be a man firmly rooted in his routines and deeply traditional. A father who will give any gift to his family. A reliable provider or a strong blue-collar father figure. He can be a materialistic person.

This card corresponds to the stoic earth religions of stillness and meditation. Religious paths that aim to let go of passions and desires and humbly contemplate the sure patterns of life. Sacrifice, sobriety, contemplation, service, and the art of becoming an empty vessel are all seen here.

II. Queen of Earth

The Queen of Earth is the hustler. She shows up every week at the market slowly gaining money throughout the day. She is a shrewd businesswoman with tons of common sense, but she is also an artist, selling what is most beautiful to her. She is strong, beautiful, and magnetic.

Card Meanings

Push harder to birth what you've envisioned and planned. Drive and follow-through are what is missing if you wish to get the money or the health that you desire.

This card could also refer to a woman (or anyone with hard-to-ignore feminine qualities, energy, or styles of dress) about to give birth to an invention, masterful art piece, or meal of some sort. Maybe she is consumed by her art and always making dolls or baking cakes. Maybe she is always making trinkets to sell or working in her garden. This is the card of a true helper. This is the card of the one who shows up to do the hard work. A workaholic. A strong mother. Big Mama, the female foundation of the blood family. A survivor and master of common sense. Able to turn scraps into a whole meal. Sometimes this card can indicate a woman pregnant with a child.

III. Prince of Earth
This Prince of Earth is a bomb ready to explode. He has the vision, the resources, the foundational home supports and has done all the planning necessary to be great. All he has to do now is carry out the spreading of the mission. Everything he wants is there. Look at him: he is sparkling and ready to travel. All he must do is jump upon his horned beast and let greatness come to him.

Card Meanings
It's time to take a trip. You have enough to take a risk. You have enough for yourself to add someone else to your project. The time for thinking is over. The initial hustle is over. It is time for you to work less and build teams. It's time to also consider marketing and what expansion looks like for your product or services. If you are asking about your

health, it's time to expand and take on new ways of eating or exercising that may even be unorthodox.

This card can be pointing to an earth boy child or a man (or anyone with hard-to-ignore boyish qualities, energy, or styles of dress) with boyish tendencies or physical tastes. This card can be someone who is extremely quick to buy too much of anything sensual, be it food, drink, cigarettes, or clothing. Addiction. This person can be into quantity of things over quality. A man who loves to hang with the boys and indulge in the pleasures of the night.

IV. Princess of Earth

I feel—the Princess of Earth spends money on what her heart desires. Sweetness guides her every step. She only moves with intuition, buying what tickles her muse. What feels good to your body? What foods make you feel free or childlike? What did you eat as a child? What sensations did you allow yourself to feel? What would you like to feel against your skin? Do you need to feel softer clothes against your skin?

Card Meanings

It is a time to be sensual. Let what feels good guide your steps. You need to taste the sweetness of life. It's not a time for strict diets or planning. Take a break.

This card can also be pointing to a young child with no sustainable connection to money, or a woman (or anyone with hard-to-ignore feminine qualities, energy, or styles of dress) with no desire to work, or a procrastinator who can't manifest what she wants. She is completely reliant on others for her support. This person indulges in the pleasure but will do none or very little of the work.

Air Kingdom

Below the mountains and far east you'll find the Air Kingdom. The Air Kingdom is known for its high-up cities and its advanced clean technology. The well-lit buildings are covered with windows, sacred geometry, solar panels, solar symbols, and paintings of high-flying birds. The beautiful streets are lined with merchants selling the most unique gadgets, trinkets, and books of puzzles, philosophy, and fine poetry. The kingdom has the smells of incense and the sounds of beeps, swooshes, and constant chatter. This is a busy town full of creatives, inventors, politicians, word-smiths, and scientists who wish to figure out every mystery and capitalize on each discovery for the advancement of humans and their comforts and also their evolution into godlike power. This Air Kingdom is full of jobs, some that matter and others not so much. Some would say that in this space, people's paths have become too many.

V. King of Air

He is firm in his thinking. His clouds are solid and holding shape. He is the King of Air and a powerful mentalist.

His maturity is high, and his discipline is unshakable. He is the wise man at the top of the windy mountain. He has recorded all that has happened. The Akashic records open wide when he comes near.

Card Meanings

What is the theme of your life? It is time to write your dogma. Organized religion or very organized clubs could be good for you. It is now time to write your book, film your movie, or get into the details of your project. You need the general structure of the entire project.

This card can represent a male (or anyone with hard-to-ignore masculine qualities, energy, or styles of dress) who is great at understanding systems and processes. This could be a man with an extremely high intellect or extremely large vocabulary. This is a card of a master strategist and higher education. This card could speak of a snobbish male who knows how smart he is. An academic or professor or a male with a high-class career such as a lawyer or a doctor. A dogmatic thinker with endless information to support his dogma.

This card can also refer to air-type religions that are focused on deep breathing, energy work, various meditations, DNA activations, and ascension into higher states of collective human consciousness.

VI. Queen of Air

The Queen of Air is reaping the benefits of all her hard work and dedication. She spent days memorizing the sixteen-page magic-bird-summoning ritual and did it perfectly after many months of hard work. She even tamed the magic bird to come at will. What do you need to focus on in order to birth the story in you? How can you enhance your own willpower to birth the invention or the story that you dreamed up?

Card Meanings

You know what you need to do. Sit down and finish it. If you have blocked out time, you must follow through for the full time you gave yourself. Increase your focus. Work on a thing only if you can dedicate at least an hour to it. Your imagination must be pushed to summon the power and spirits and ideas that you really need.

Beware of logical conclusions based on faulty root systems. A logical conclusion can land far from a good target if the linear trajectory was propelled from a shaky archer. The logical answer is not always correct. Logic without the heart is not truly rational. To trust the ends of rushed linear conclusions can bring trouble.

This is most likely a woman (or anyone with hard-to-ignore feminine qualities, energy, or styles of dress) who is incredibly smart and witty or focused. She is all discipline, putting nothing above her goals. A relentless teacher or mentor who is obsessed with perfection. A woman who can push her mind beyond the limitations of her body. A stubborn woman who is always right and can't be stopped. A female who has the discipline to carry out any task. A strict accountability partner. A philosopher and over-thinker. An overly critical mother.

VII. Prince of Air

The Prince of Air is flying on a creature created in the depths of his mother's mind. The people don't all approve. Some say it's witchcraft; some say he's using illusions to be deceitful and scare the people. What are the people saying about the thoughts that you share? Are you letting their opinions destroy your visions or propel you into greatness? Everyone already knows. It's okay; and if they don't know, they should. Don't hide from anyone. You can handle the blowback.

Card Meanings

Let other people judge your project, and be open to critique. Release the project. Perhaps you've been like a mother trying to hold onto your work. It needs to be tested. Put it out there. Say what you need to say. No secrets. Secrets will not last. Stand firm in your truth.

This card could represent a child prodigy or a young man (or anyone with hard-to-ignore masculine qualities, energy, or styles of dress) obsessed with games or gaming. A technology addict. A young man obsessed with hip-hop or writing or telling crazy stories. The card could represent a liar or someone who gossips or tells tall tales.

This is a card of someone who overshares information and can't keep secrets. This is the card of the riddler, the boy or man who plays too many games. A man who changes his mind easily.

VIII. Princess of Air

The Princess of Air is concerned only with fresh new ways of thinking. When she isn't daydreaming, her mind is completely open to knowledge. She meditates on a cloud deep in her own mind. If she were to fall, she would only land upon a giant bird provided by the King and Queen. She is fully free to indulge in whatever muse comes to her. Being led by the muse, she is not loyal to any ideas or any of her commitments.

Card Meanings

Don't fixate on any one thought. Relax. You will find what you are looking for when you forget about it. Be carefree. What wants to come to you? Wait for the muses. Only go in the direction that you are inspired to go. There is no need to commit to anything. The world is so big and full of various ways of thinking. Why focus on one? Does that even sound interesting?

This card could be indicating an air-sign child or girl (or anyone with hard-to-ignore youthful feminine qualities, energy, or styles of dress) who lives completely in her ideals. A young girl who is incredibly easy to influence. A fickle girl who jumps from one thing to the next. A young poet. A woman who keeps secrets.

Fire Kingdom

The Fire Kingdom of the south is a vibrant place full of huge festivals, delicious foods, dancing, street performers, and lights. There isn't a street where music can't be heard. Even in the farthest reaches, a faint banging of drums or a screeching trumpet will always keep one company. The temptations are everywhere, and flirtation is life. Lovers run about holding hands, racing from one event to the next. Children can also be seen holding candies and playing tag while friendly untamed animals run among them. The Fire Kingdom is a land of joy and entertainment. Even the priests show up at the festivities in garments of various bright colors and special fabrics. The kingdom doesn't sleep, and its inhabitants love it that way. The land is also known for its fierce warrior class and commands the most respect in war times.

IX. King of Fire

The King of Fire is the high chief of the Royal Court cards. The fiery military general of the bush has a full-fledged military hidden among the trees, ready for any battles that may come his way. He is also an amazing orator who is able to keep his troops inspired with vision and purpose.

Card Meanings

Get your life in order. Take full charge; it's time to lead.

The King of Fire might represent the leader of a town. A person who listens to the will of the people and speaks up for them. He is fearless. He is not concerned with how he is perceived, because he is one with his vision and firmly grounded in values that resonate with the people. His only concern is to burn bright for his passion and vision. He can't be bought or swayed with money. This person could be a husband who leads a family into victory and much success!

This card can also refer to a fire-type religion, which is any religion focused on spreading its message through igniting a fire in the souls of others. Lively music, charismatic teaching, faith healing, and people shouting and praising can be seen in many of these religious traditions.

X. Queen of Fire

The Queen of Fire stands strong with a fist in the air. She is fully possessed by the warrior spirits of her ancestry. The pressure is on, but she has so much experience in fighting that the pressures that surround her can't dictate her next moves. She has a huge community that will do anything for her. She can take them deep into trance states in full alignment with her focus and purity of heart.

Card Meanings
Pine tree energy. This is a strong card for resistance and perseverance in the face of adversity.

Passion, dance, spirit possession, channeling strong forces. Push hard. Stand strong. Stronger plant medicines could help release through purging.

The Queen of Fire could manifest as a woman (or anyone with hard-to-ignore feminine qualities, energy, or styles of dress) with a zeal for travel and exploring. She may also be a woman with a huge personality that just can't be ignored. She is a woman with a strong instinct who moves in alignment with her gut. A strong mother who can see through lies. A medicine woman or a supporter of community and family.

This card correlates to types of magic that change the circumstances of the user. For people looking for money, or a mate, to win a trial, or for their cheating partner to change their ways, this is the type of magic they are looking for.

XI. Prince of Fire
The Prince of Fire is on a high mission from the Creator. Nothing will stop the spread of his vision. It's time for campaigning to begin. The movement is ready to sweep

through the streets like a fire. Travel, and talk with your heart to the masses. They've been waiting for this day.

Card Meanings
Large ceremony, spread of ideas to the masses, group think, many moving with one accord. Taking huge risks.

The Prince of Fire could be a young man (or anyone with hard-to-ignore boyish qualities, energy, or styles of dress) who is always placing himself in danger. He could be running with gangs or doing tricks on his dirt bike. He lives for a thrill and will take any chance to experience that rush. A person who always takes credit or has a hard time sharing a stage. This card could represent someone with a hard time sticking to one passion. A person who hops from school to school based on his quickly changing interests. A person who thinks he can handle all things on his own. A flashy young man.

XII. Princess of Fire
The Princess of Fire is available. She is open to being of service to those in need. What she lacks in ability, she makes up for with heart and bright spirits. The wise can see her, but she wishes to be seen by the masses someday. Perhaps when she gets older she will have more tools to be heard. A bright and joyous child who brings laughter to those who are close, she is a treasure to her small circle.

Card Meanings

Help someone. Let someone else's vision inspire your own.

The Princess of Fire could manifest as someone who has a lot of heart but needs support.

Someone with a disability or someone really young. Someone with an important message that needs a microphone or a stage. This could be someone with a great idea that no one has noticed. This card could represent someone who needs a voice.

Water Kingdom

Legend has it that the ancestors of the Water Kingdom descended from shape-shifting mermaids who brought the secrets of real magic to the surface. The kingdom lines the western shores where waves crash against banks. Cloaked figures can be seen performing various magical rites at night in the dark forest. The honor for the gods of old is high in the land: no tree is cut nor forest hunted without consulting the nature spirits. They reside in the fluids of the leaves and roots, the blood of animals, and the oceans. Therefore, all the high priests are of the waters. In the daytime, you can find many of the families fishing in lakes, harvesting medicinal plants in the forest, or joyfully riding beautiful boats off the shore. The shadows of legendary sea creatures who protect the people can at times be seen under the boats.

XIII. King of Water

The King of Water loves the surface of the water. He is often seen elegantly riding on the backs of dolphins while taking in large breaths of air. His connection to the air element represents his love for the intellect. As much as he rules water, he never wishes to get lost in his own waters. He will never be lost in his emotions, but he will allow himself to feel them and then quickly categorize where they belong in relation to his thoughts. He wishes to love the waters but to also protect himself and the people he loves from the dangers within it.

Card Meanings

Gather your thoughts around your emotions. What is your protocol for when emotions take over? It is time to manage those emotions and place them where they belong. The magic is in the moment, but the truth and protection are in the patterns. Don't harp on any emotion for too long. You don't have time to be complacent.

This card is often a counselor or a sound, reciprocal husband (or any good-hearted person with hard-to-ignore masculine qualities, energy, or styles of dress). This is the nice and playful father who might cook and clean and loves children. This father is a storyteller who can tap into the emotions of everyone around him. His stories are solid and deeply penetrating into the heart of his children. This card refers to a man truly in tune with the divine feminine. He is not afraid to cry and appreciates deep beauty. He has found a way to also balance his creativity in such a way that he is able to make money from what is dear to his heart. He is a kind and loving partner. Sometimes this person does not have money, but he can bring emotional stability to the household. He is a sound male who is deeply sensitive and intuitive. He has a ton of great qualities, but he is not fond of fighting. He would rather avoid conflict.

This card can also represent the ancient water religions that worship nature or natural spirits with the use of shrines, rituals, animal offerings, or herbs. The spirits of these religions need the waters of earth to stay energized enough to work for us: the magic red waters of the properly slain animal, the fresh, vibrant water-filled and sometimes crushed herbs, certain oils, and the "fire water" known as alcohol.

XIV. Queen of Water

The Queen of Water rules the deep. She is the divine mermaid swimming through your dreams trying to lead you to your deepest and most precious spiritual powers. There is baggage that must be cleared and emotional pain that must be freed. She is the wild subconscious sleep that nourishes your body while your astral body is processing your waking emotions.

Card Meanings

Process those deep emotions through the arts or spiritual ceremony. A personal ritual could allow for a gentle purging of sorrows. Focus on that emotion and work deeply with it. This is not the time to bury that emotion. It is time to find that emotion and magnify it with tools. Go into that emotion ready to face the ugly and see it for what it is without judging yourself. Do the hard work. Wrestle with it through writing, meditation, painting, dancing, or just sitting and allowing yourself to feel it truly before doing anything. You can't rush the process.

This card also says that emotion is a creator. Logical conclusions aren't enough right now to make the magic happen. If your mind is there and your heart isn't, you will fail. It is most beneficial to wrestle your way out of the mind and activate your life. Even if the path makes no sense to your rational mind, the heart is correct.

The queen can manifest as the guru who challenges your most cherished beliefs. This card can also represent the wailing women (or folks with hard-to-ignore feminine qualities, energy, or styles of dress) who cry and pray for the widow, the orphan, and the sick. This is the card of the prayer warrior and also the seer who receives downloads from the realms of the unseen. She has premonitions while asleep and wakes up to jot them all down. The divine has a hand on her, and she is completely tuned into the people in her circle. She will make sure that they do not process those emotions alone. She could also pop up as an oracle, a medium, or a maker of herbal teas for the soul. A mature soul is easily able to see reflection and hold oneself accountable when things pop up in community.

XV. Prince of Water

The Prince of Water has stepped out of the waters to bring his message to the surface. He is singing his love songs and doing his dance and proclaiming his deep emotional message. It all matters so much to him. He doesn't care if people understand his huge heart. He just wants someone to feel him and to love him unconditionally.

Card Meanings

Let others know how you feel. Bring out your artistic skills for the world to see. You are ready for love. Go out and place yourself into a religious temple or community festivities or activity clubs and know that the Creator will begin to connect you to a good mate for you. If you are in a relationship, it could be a great time to propose.

This card could manifest as a ladies' man or any masculine romance fanatic. He falls in love extremely fast and can also fall out of love fast once the muse leaves him. He is always chasing his dream girl, usually realizing that he was only projecting upon someone he can't settle down with. He is easily pulled into temptation but can also be an exceptionally fun and romantic lover. He could represent a new boyfriend or a guy that will help you to get over the one that you left. He's most likely not here to stay. He could also be a musician or an artist of some sort.

XVI. Princess of Water

The Princess of Water swims from one magical fantasy to the next. She is completely detached from the worries of the world. She is a fun hunter. She is not concerned with patterns, only moments. She is fully aware that the magic is in the moment.

Card Meanings

Take it easy and feed your inner child. It is okay to break your routine.

The Princess of Water can oftentimes refer to a baby, especially a baby girl. She could also refer to any super feminine person of exceptional beauty who is deeply into their external appearance. This card could refer to someone who has an extremely young way of dealing with emotions and deals with a great jealousy. This person may be extremely clingy and needy and unable to make decisions.

ABOUT THE AUTHOR

Monticue Connally is an author, Afrofuturist, herbalist, oracle reader, plant medium, medicine man, and father of four. Herbs, medical astrology, tarot, orishas, sacred objects, African spirituality, singing, and alternative healing methods have been lifelong interests for the longtime Denver resident who currently lives on the island of Barbados, where he continues to study, teach, explore, and raise his family with his wife, a local sangoma healer.

He has taught for the Denver Botanic Gardens Herbalism Certificate Program and now teaches for the Colorado School of Clinical Herbalism. He also served for a time as lead herbalist and youth coordinator for the FrontLine Farming organization. He received the Preventive Care Leadership Award from the Be Well Health and Wellness Initiative in 2019 for being of service to diverse Black and brown communities, pushing them toward the accessible and immediate plant medicines growing all around them.

Deeply spiritual and sensitive to subtle energies, Monticue has found great pleasure in the art of tree talking and working with the spirits of the roots, which ground, energize, protect, and bring great joy to his life.

Instagram: @monticue_the_herbalist • Facebook: facebook.com/monticue.connally • Patreon: Patreon.com/arootawakening

SPECIAL THANK YOU

The author would like to thank the staff at North Atlantic Books, Jonathon Stalls, Sharona Thompson, Mustapha Major, Dani Otteson, Marian Kellog, Roosevelt Price, and all those who contributed any amount of advice or support as I brainstormed and moved through writing this book.